Tribute to *Heroes in O*

My wife and I thoroughly enjoyed Jim's accounts of his life as a Naval Officer and he ranks at the top of the "Heroes" list for service to his country. His insight and observations are dead center of what really matters in the military: devotion, sacrifice, diligence, and unwavering loyalty to the men serving with him. This is a book that had to be written and Jim has done it so well, the curtains of "Obscurity" totally disappear. It is a tribute to unsung American sailors in the Vietnam era, a collection of light-hearted tales and a fun, while informative, read. Valuable history from a Christian viewpoint.

Jack L. Drain
Lt/Col USAF Ret.
Author: *Life on a Short Fuse*

Heroes in Obscurity is a sincere, joyful look at a U.S. Navy officer's service on "least of these" classes of ships during the Vietnam era. As a lifelong friend, and fellow naval officer, I applaud Jim on his memories of our days as shipboard junior officers. While my service was defined by much different assignments, Jim's service allowed him a unique and humorous set of experiences that can be best enjoyed in microcosmic surroundings. Thanks, Jim, for telling a valuable story of service that would otherwise be forgotten and certainly lost in annals that are fixated on flashy, big stories.

John C. Williams
Captain U.S.N. Ret.

It is clear that Jim Duermeyer loved his active duty years in the U.S. Navy. His memory of that time is sharp, and his stories of those years are very engaging. Whether the reader is an armchair warrior or one who has served, or is serving, this book offers a candid, humble and humorous account of a young naval officer's experiences at sea and ashore while obtaining his qualifications for greater rank and responsibility. Jim Duermeyer served on three active duty ships, ships that were not large or famous, ships that did their actual hard work every day, ships that caused young officers to mature rapidly. The reader will delight in the author's tales from these unsung, rather obscure ships of the world's strongest navy, written carefully to emphasize the human details that brought variety, vitality, and joy to a naval officer's young career.

Stephen P. Duermeyer
Captain U.S.N. Ret.

MILITARY MONOGRAPH 128

Heroes in Obscurity

A Vietnam Era Junior Officer's Stories of Unsung Heroes and of Life on Small Navy Auxiliary Ships

CDR James Duermeyer
USNR-Ret

Bennington, Vermont
2011

— Heroes in Obscurity —

First published in 2011 by the Merriam Press

First Edition

Copyright © 2011 by James Duermeyer
Book design by Ray Merriam
Additional material copyright of named contributors.

The views expressed are solely those of the author.

ISBN 978-1-257-80503-7 (paperback) #MM128-P
ISBN 978-1-257-84905-5 (hardcover) #MM128-H

Printed in the United States of America.

This work was designed, produced, and published in
the United States of America by the

Merriam Press
133 Elm Street Suite 3R
Bennington VT 05201

E-mail: ray@merriam-press.com
Web site: merriam-press.com

Both the author and the Publisher welcome and encourage
comments and corrections to the material appearing in this work.
Please send them to the Publisher at the above address.

The Merriam Press is always interested in publishing new manuscripts on
military history, as well as reprinting previous works, such as reports, documents,
manuals, articles and other material on military history topics.

Dedication

TO the millions of men and women who came forward and selflessly answered the call by their nation to serve in the military during the Vietnam War era, and especially those who served in unglorious, obscure positions to aid the brave front-line warriors. You are indeed, Heroes in Obscurity.

Contents

Foreword

"People sleep peaceably in their beds at night only because rough men stand ready to do violence on their behalf."
—*Author unknown*

THERE were 8.7 million of us.[1] We came from every city, town, and village across the United States. We came in response to a call from our country. The call came in the involuntary form of a letter, or it came from the heart of the participant. But the results were the same. We naïve young men and women would answer the call to bear arms for our nation in its conflict with communism in the heretofore little known country of Vietnam.

When the millions stepped forward, none knew what was ahead as they entered their respective military careers. They entered various branches of the service, either voluntarily, or involuntarily. But the subsequent tasks assigned to them determined the degree of danger, hard work, and responsibility they would encounter. Many would be assigned to support positions. And many others would face the horrific, indescribable scenes of face-to-face combat with the enemy. More than one hundred fifty-three thousand would be wounded seriously enough to require hospitalization,[2] and fifty-eight thousand one hundred and forty-eight[3] would pay the ultimate price for their bravery and for that call from their country.

Every five years I attend my small high school class reunion. At each reunion the veterans are asked to come forward for a group photo. I am amazed at the number of veterans in my class. Vietnam veterans make up 9.7% of our generation.[4] Yet, almost half of the hundred plus young men in my high school class served in the military during the Vietnam era, with a large percentage of them having served in the Vietnam Theater. I get a lump in my throat each time I go to that reunion, and I am extremely proud of each of them. To think they each gave up a minimum of two years of their lives to serve their country in a time of need, in an unpopu-

---

[1] *World Almanac and Book of Facts 2009*, World Almanac Books.
[2] Ibid.
[3] Ibid.
[4] The Long Way Home Project: Statistics and References, http://www.longwayhome.net/references.htm#uniform.

lar war, is amazing to me. All of these veteran classmates are unsung heroes to me, no matter where they served.

Of the thousands who came forward between 1964 and 1973 to serve in the Vietnam War, by far the toughest job was to be on the ground in Vietnam facing a strong, militaristically skilled, and smart enemy. The men in those positions never knew from one day to the next if they would live or die. Each of those men is a special American hero, deserving of our undying respect.

Many books have been written about the ground campaign in Vietnam. And there have been books about the "brown water Navy" serving in Vietnam. The bulk of the Vietnam books are about the "tip of the spear" operations—the units which were forward-deployed and met the enemy head on. In all branches of the military, these up-front units make the headlines, and, rightfully so, earn the most awards and recognition. I salute the accomplishments and bravery of these extraordinary groups of men and women. This book is most emphatically not meant to take away any of the huge sacrifice of the front line military.

But what about the thousands of men (and women) who volunteered, or were drafted, and did not serve in front line units? Although they did not meet the enemy head on, their jobs in support of the men on the front line deserve discussion and merit, and they are also deserving of credit equal to that given to front line units. These individuals served in a multitude of sometimes boring, mundane, unglorious jobs that were necessary to support the front line warriors. They may have served as a clerk at a desk, a driver, a mechanic, a barber, or a cook. They may have served as postal clerks, supply clerks, religious leaders, or fork lift operators. One of my friends spent his entire Vietnam era service playing the tuba in an Army band. I chuckle at that assignment, but at least he answered the call to arms. All branches of the military had such positions. My anecdotal stories narrate the contributions of a small group of unsung Navy men during the Vietnam era, and pay a small, well deserved tribute to these hard working sailors.

I heard it said once that of all the branches of the military, the Navy receives far less recognition than that accorded to the other branches, especially in the type of conflict being fought in the Middle East today. Assuming this to be true, the Navy continues its specialized business in the war effort without a great deal of fanfare.

In the "haze gray and underway" Navy, there are the forward-deployed combatant ships, such as the destroyers, cruisers, and aircraft carriers. But there is also a category of ships built specifically to provide support to units on the front line. In the Navy's case, that front line could be on land, at sea, or in the air. These support ships provide services to any of those fronts, and to their forward-deployed brothers, the combatant ships of the line. These supporting ships, at least during the Vietnam era, were classified and called service ships, or auxiliary ships. But to the unsung heroes who served on them, they will always be referred to as "the working Navy!" Because of their mission and status, "Heroes in Obscurity" aptly describes the important roles these units played in the working Navy.

I had the pleasure of serving on three such U.S. Navy ships during the Vietnam War era. Two of these ships were based in Charleston, South Carolina, and the third ship, in which I saw duty in Vietnam, was based at Pearl Harbor. Many of my stories will relate to that third ship, the USS Ute (ATF-76), a fleet salvage tug, classified as an auxiliary ship, operating in and out of South Vietnam ports during the conflict.

For many years I have thought that my unglamorous Vietnam story and anecdotal adventures might warrant a written compilation. A relative advised me that I would need to make the book "sexy." In other words, spice it up to make it more exciting. Not only is that not necessarily in my nature, but it is not the purpose of this book. There is no fighting or battles, nor is there any outwardly recognized glory in this book. My purpose is to relate some of my adventures (and some misadventures) while serving beside a small group of unsung Navy heroes onboard service ships during the Vietnam War, from my viewpoint as a lowly junior commissioned officer.

To aid in telling the stories from my perspective, the book begins with some personal background. I believe this section will reveal the human side of the thoughts and life-changing decisions that faced all young men in this time period. The stories of shipboard life follow the introduction. This is a group of stories of some unsung heroes, unceremoniously toiling aboard mostly unknown naval ships, doing unglamorous and extremely hard work in support of the "tip of the spear." In the case of these Navy men, they volunteered to place themselves in harm's way, answering the call from their country. These unsung heroes truly worked in obscurity.

I write this collection of anecdotes based on as much fact as I recall. I have taken some liberties in telling the stories to make them more interesting, readable, and a bit humorous. I have changed the names of characters in the stories, and the quotations used in the book are not exact. Quotes reflect incidents to the best of my memory and heighten continuity of the stories. And finally, the jokes interspersed throughout the book are from anonymous, unknown sources on the internet and are widely available in public domain. Among many good sources for Navy jokes, one is author Jeff Edwards' web site, www.navythriller.com. The jokes I have used in my stories, and many other Navy jokes, are widely available at many sites on the internet.

I hope you will enjoy this collection of non-combat stories of life aboard the unglorious, yet hard working, Navy ships on which I served during the Vietnam era.

Introduction

THE year is 1964. With a war raging half-way around the world in Southeast Asia and an active Selective Service draft in force, almost all able-bodied young men in the United States in 1964, and thereafter until 1973, would sooner or later be wearing a military uniform. The question was not whether you would soon be wearing a uniform; but rather, whether or not you waited to be drafted, or whether you volunteered to enter the military. It was almost inevitable that draftees would be called into the Army. If a young man did not wish to enter the Army, the alternative was volunteering to enter another branch of service which had a mission or theater of operations that was more appealing.

The Selective Service Act was created in 1940 by President Franklin Roosevelt, and it was still in effect at the beginning, and continued until the end, of the Vietnam War.[5] The Act required that every young man, upon reaching his eighteenth birthday, report to his local county courthouse and register for the draft. The resultant list of young men from across the nation was then used to fill the ranks of primarily our nation's Army, but in some cases also helped with the staffing of the U.S. Marines. In 1969, the Selective Service System under President Nixon initiated a nationwide lottery system, which picked birthdates for filling quotas for men by the military.[6] I was already in the military when the first lottery numbers were drawn.

I turned 18 in February of 1964, and like all young men at the time, I reported to my local county office of the Selective Service and signed up for the draft. We really did not understand the significance of that procedure, until later. We also did not know many, if any, of our peers who had gone before us into the military. We were carefree in our senior year of high school and paid little attention to our first step toward the military. However, upon graduation the significance and the resultant reality of signing up for the draft became abruptly apparent for many of my classmates. Many were drafted and entered the Army immediately, serving in the Southeast Asia Theater, with several of them seeing combat duty on the front lines of the Vietnam fire fights.

---

[5] Selective Service System, History and Records, http://www.sss.gov/backgr.htm.
[6] Selective Service System, History and Records, http://www.sss.gov/lotter2.htm.

For me school was just something that had to be done. Studying was something that the "smart kids" did, and I found it all a bit boring. Surprisingly, I was able to maintain decent grades (however less than stellar,) even though at this point in my life I was not focusing on my abilities. I liked the camaraderie of my friends, and I even liked some of my courses. Being a skinny little runt, I was a track miler and a cross country runner. And I was very active in music. I was a soloist in the choir and played first chair French horn in the high school band and orchestra. Although I did not consider myself a scholar, it was expected of me by my teachers and my parents that I would attend college.

After high school, I, and many of my classmates, moved on to attend colleges and universities. If we remained in college, the Selective Service granted us a "2S" deferment from being drafted into the Army. An individual could hold a 2S classification for a maximum of four years. At the end of the four years, an individual was subject to the draft.

My college entrance scores were excellent and my grades, while not great, allowed me to be accepted at all three Iowa public universities. I chose the University of Iowa, and another chapter of my life began. My freshman year at Iowa was fun. And sadly, that is about all it was. I was not yet mature enough to focus on the main purpose for being in Iowa City. I was a fraternity guy having a good time with dating, parties, and very little studying. As a result, my grades suffered in that first year, and although I could have returned to campus the following fall, I was extremely ashamed and angry at myself.

During summer break, my parents met with me in Minnesota, where I was working as a counselor and water-front instructor at a boy's camp, and we had a lengthy, heated discussion about what road my future should follow. I convinced them that I wanted to stay in school, but that I would like to return to our home town and attend William Penn University in Oskaloosa, Iowa. My parents were against this transfer, but in the end they agreed. I transferred to William Penn University in Oskaloosa and began working almost full time at the local J.C. Penney store to help pay for my college expenses. Not only was I more easily able to help pay for my education, but the smaller classes and more intense study in this smaller university helped me focus, and my grades rose accordingly.

In my third year of college, several significant things happened. First, the Vietnam War, half a globe away in Southeast Asia, continued with an unending need for young men in the military. I would need to make a decision on how I would fulfill my military obligation. When in doubt, ask for advice.

I went to my older brother, Steve, whom I have always looked up to, attempted to emulate, and like all younger brothers, believed him to be "cool" and almost invincible. Four years older than I, he graduated from high school and college four years ahead of me. After college, he attended Navy Officer Candidate School, received his commission, and served shipboard, carrying out "Market Time" duties off the coast of Vietnam. Market Time was a process used during the Vietnam War, whereby U.S. Navy vessels intercepted Vietnamese maritime traffic to search the boats for contraband and/or human cargo that could be used by North Vietnam. Steve would continue his career with the Navy and retire at the rank of captain after thirty years of service. In that time, he commanded several ships, including two very large auxiliary ships, the USS Suribachi (AE-21), an ammunition ship; and the USS Wabash (AOR-5), a replenishment oiler. As my older brother, and because he was deeply involved in his own Navy auxiliary ship adventure, he is one of my unsung heroes.

Earlier, my brother and I had discussed my options. Naturally, because he was already a naval officer, he pushed me toward the same objective. And of course, because he was the older brother I looked up to, the plan was set.

In those days, you could sign up for Officer Candidate School two years ahead of your college graduation. And the two years before you graduated would count as time served in the Navy for pay purposes. Essentially, you would enter Officer Candidate School at a higher pay bracket than those who waited until after graduation. So, during my junior year of college, I traveled to Des Moines, Iowa, raised my right hand before an officer recruiter and signed up to report to Navy Officer Candidate School following college graduation. The path had been finalized and unbeknownst to me, I would end up wearing a Navy officer's military uniform for twenty years.

Another important incident in my junior year of college occurred one day while I was strolling down the hall of the main academic building at William Penn University. The Dean of the college spied me, and we started chatting. He asked me what I was majoring in and what courses I was taking. I told him that I had always had an interest in psychology and thought that would be a good major. I had already taken twenty four hours of psychology courses. The Dean then informed me that the college did not have a psychology major. Pause—this is one of those, Oh Crap moments (substitute other wording if you like). They seemed to happen to me quite often. But being the academic wizard for the campus, the Dean proceeded to pull out the course catalog and began comparing it to the courses I had already taken. I watched in worried anticipation, because with my financial position and my commitment to the Navy, I needed to complete college in four years. The Dean continued grinding through the courses I had taken, adding all the hours, comparing his results to the school course catalog, and finally said, "Duermeyer, you need to take some summer school courses, and you will graduate with a major that will include a social science composite with an emphasis in business and a minor in psychology." Well, how about that. With the help of the college dean, I now had a college major, and I was only in the middle of my junior year.

The most significant event that happened in my third year of college was that I was introduced to the wonderful girl who would become my wife. Janet was from northwest Iowa and was excelling at her studies in order to complete college at Minnesota State University Mankato in three years. OK, OK, I give her credit for having the brains in our family, and she's a sweetie besides. We still laugh about how we met. But that is another whole story. I sincerely believe that God brought two very different people together for a blind date and enjoyed watching the humorous interaction between two very unlikely matched people. But the broader purpose was that God knew I was still immersed in my youthful ways. I still was unfocused and seemed to be running in neutral many times. After a time of long distance dating and professing my love to Janet, and she to me, my life changed for the better. An example is that my grades in college soon became all A's and B's. I also became aware that I was finally going to graduate from college, that I was going to be a naval officer after college, and that I would have the best partner I could ever ask for to accompany me on my further life adventures. When I asked Janet to be my bride, I also told her that I was pretty sure that I would make the Navy my career. This would mean a great deal of moving around, and a lot of separations while I spent shipboard time at sea on deployments. I told Janet that I would understand if she did not want to marry me. But Janet thinks a lot like I do, and she said that she looked forward to being a Navy wife and traveling around the world. She agreed to be married. Janet and I are still best friends after 42 years of marriage, and we continue living our lives together, doing the best we can through our remaining years.

Part One

Preparation for Sea Duty

Having passed the enlistment physical, Henry was asked by the doctor, "Why do you want to join the Navy, son?" Henry replied, "My father said it'd be a good idea, Sir." "Oh, and what does your father do?" said the doctor. "He's in the Army, Sir!"
—Author unknown

September 1968—Officer Candidate School (OCS), Newport, R.I.

A close friend, John, had likewise struggled with the post-college military decision. We had gone through elementary, middle, and high school together. His family and mine went to the same church, and they lived a few houses down from us on the same street in Oskaloosa, Iowa. He and I participated in some of the same activities in school and had many of the same interests; however, he was much more studious than I. John and I went to different colleges, but we stayed in touch. As we both considered our military options, it turned out that he had reached the same conclusion I had and was accepted to Navy Officer Candidate School in Newport, where we were scheduled to enter at the same time. How great, somebody to commiserate with while facing OCS.

To commemorate college graduation, I received a firm handshake from my dad and best wishes from my mom, while John was presented a brand new Oldsmobile Cutlass coupe. How cool is that! We would ride to Newport, Rhode Island, in style.

The day of our departure arrived, and the two of us drove away to become naval officers. Prior to leaving, John's father counseled him not to try to drive all the way to Newport from Iowa. He said we should swap out the driving duties and stop overnight somewhere along the way to get some sleep. Now, my friend John is a very fastidious fellow, and he was bursting with pride over that new Olds. Although I volunteered to relieve him at the wheel, I quickly ascertained that he was not about to let me drive his new "baby," and he remained at the wheel for hour after hour as we motored east. I understood his over-protective attitude toward his new car. We spent the night in an interstate motel and the next morning, with about four or five hours of sleep, we jumped back into the Olds, and continued on to Newport.

At that time, my brother Steve was stationed aboard a destroyer escort at Newport as the Engineering Officer. He had rented and was living in the gatehouse of one of the Newport mansions. When we arrived in Newport, we went to his apartment and crashed with him. We would begin OCS in a couple days, so we had time to rest up and look around

Newport. It is a beautiful, picturesque city, with a long and colorful maritime history.

The city of Newport dates back to its founding in 1639. The first settlers, who were Quakers and Jews, established an agricultural community. By the late 1600s Newport was one of the five largest cities in America. In the 1700s, it had established itself as a maritime community, and shipbuilding was its major industry. Newport was also a center in slave trade, rum production, and piracy. But by 1815, the city had lost its industry, and the locale became the Mecca for the moneyed folks to build their unbelievable mansions.[7]

The Continental Navy used Newport extensively during the Revolutionary War, and Newport has had a Navy presence there since that time. The port was a busy center during the Civil War, and the Naval Academy at Annapolis was temporarily moved to Newport for fear that it would be taken over by the confederacy. In the 1880s, the Navy began actively building a multitude of training facilities on Narragansett Bay, and it was around this time that the famous torpedo factory on Goat Island was established. In 1884, the Naval War College was established. As a major naval training facility, thousands of Navy recruits were trained in Newport for both the first and second world wars. John F. Kennedy received his P.T. boat training at the Naval Base. The Naval Officer Candidate School, the Navy's primary source of Naval Reserve Officers, began in 1951. It was moved briefly to Pensacola, Florida, but later returned to Newport where it resides today.[8] With my OCS experience there and having visited Newport many times since, I consider Newport to be one of my favorite places.

After two days of playing tourist, John and I drove to the Navy base and followed directions to the OCS parking lot for new officer candidates. We parked the car, walked to the back, and opened the trunk. We had both brought our golf clubs, hoping to play some golf on what we thought would be leisurely weekends. So, those golf clubs were the first things we reached for in emptying the trunk. But just as we set them on the ground and were reaching for our suitcases, we heard someone yell,

"Hey cockroaches, what do you think you are doing with golf clubs?" Cockroaches?

We both looked around and discovered that the voice belonged to some guy in a pseudo Navy officer's uniform, and he was yelling at us. I thought the answer to that was pretty obvious. We were going to play some golf in our free time.

---

[7] *Rhode Island 101*, Tim Lehnert, MacIntyre Purcell Publishing, Inc., 2009.
[8] Naval Station Newport, History, http://www.mybaseguide.com/navy/newport/.

This obnoxious, moronic yelling person continued, "You cockroaches are not going to need any damn golf clubs while you are at OCS. Put them back in the car. And you are not going to see this car for a long time. Lock the car, get your suitcases, and follow me! C'mon, c'mon, make it snappy, cockroaches."

We found out later that cockroaches was an endearing term for first quarter, new officer candidates, and we would hear that term a lot, referring to us. Thus began the first month of Navy Officer Candidate School and the hazing and discipline that followed. We learned that we were "lower than a cockroach's belly, more putrid than dead octopi, and dumber than whale excrement."

The prospective officer candidates, aka cockroaches, were gathered together as a group, each assigned to a company, and "stumble marched" to the barracks to drop off our suitcases. We were then herded off to pick up uniforms and have all of our hair cut off. So far, OCS did not seem to be very much fun.

During the first five days of OCS, we were not allowed to sleep through the night, calisthenics were held nearly every hour, inspections were held every four or five hours, and physicals were held along with numerous inoculations for who knew what diseases. Most of us were dragging and miserable at the end of the week. It was the lack of sleep during that first week that I remember most. It was unpleasant, to say the least, and the actual instructional classes had not even started! At this point, all of this fun was being administered by upper classmen. We later found out that they had volunteered for "hell week" in order to take the civilian out of our characters. Sadistic devils. Their happy little activities appeared to be successful, as we began more and more to learn "the Navy way."

In the second week, classes began. There were classes in Navy organization, ship tactics, communications, seamanship, physical training, navigation, damage control training, even more physical training, and other subjects I do not recall. Our classroom instructors were either Navy officers or Navy chief petty officers. The officers were generally lieutenants, and the chiefs were either senior or master chiefs. In addition to the classroom instructors, each company was assigned an active duty lieutenant as the company officer. This lieutenant was to be a sort of mentor, and a resource for any questions or problems that might occur within the officer candidate ranks of the company. Our lieutenant was a really nice guy, who assisted us with our questions and our routine. Generally, the instructors and company lieutenants were helpful, because many of them had gone through the same process we were experiencing.

But once in a while an officer or chief might want to have some fun at your expense.

The Marching Machine

We marched so much that we began to believe that every time we flipped a calendar page it still said March! (ouch, sorry)

Our days were scheduled down to the minute, and we marched in formation as a company to every scheduled activity. Consequently, during the first couple of weeks, we practiced marching almost every day after classes to become proficient. Our rag-tag group of college graduate officer wannabes were designated Echo Company.

After a week or so, my friend John was appointed as company commander, and I was appointed the company guide-on. The guide-on marches at the front of the company, carrying a long pole with the company flag at the top. Everyone marching behind me could see the pole and flag that I carried. When the company commander would shout out a marching order, the guide-on would lift the pole with its flag, and smartly bring it back down so that all members of the company knew when to implement the order. When the pole went up, it meant get ready. When it came down, it was time to execute the order. It was kind of a fun job, and because I had my hands full with the guide-on pole, somebody marching behind me in the company always had to carry my text books.

We even marched to the chow hall in formation. We would wait outside the chow hall until other companies had eaten and there was room for us to move into the chow hall. This usually worked well, until winter in Newport really kicked in. In December and January the wind would churn an icy blast across Narragansett Bay. On the days when the temperature approached zero, with a wind off the bay of thirty miles an hour, we were chilled to the bone and half frozen as we waited in the icy blast for as much as a half hour until we could enter the chow hall. On those days, we all vehemently cursed the Navy and the "military way."

Being in a closed, closely watched environment like OCS, it is often hard to find humor and have fun. One day, I had an opportunity to help our company commander see a bit of human reality and have a little fun too. We were marching to class, and as we did so, we passed by classroom buildings and other companies as they marched to their destinations. Suddenly, John gave a command to march to the right. I knew this was an incorrect order, as we would end up marching into a wall. But the devil in me just wouldn't let me pass up this opportunity. As soon as he gave the order to execute the right turn, I followed the order, lowered the guide-on and turned right and marched the company into the side of a building. After banging into the side of the building, I continued to march in place while everyone piled up behind me. In the meantime, other companies were marching past, and some Navy officer instructors watched this scene with amusement from the entrance to their nearby buildings. I was thoroughly enjoying this, and I looked around at the other members in the company, and they all had their heads down suppressing their laughter. The company commander finally got us back into formation and marching ahead to class. But I could sure see that John's bubble had burst, and he was not at all happy, especially with me. Ah, well, I was only following orders. There were a few other humorous marching incidents, but even with the missteps, our company was a pack of marching aficionados.

John was a great company commander, and our marching became proficient. We knew we were good, and it would pay off for us, as you will see in a moment. As a side note, my friend John stayed with the Navy and made it his career. He distinguished himself with his performance, was assigned many highly responsible assignments including Naval Attaché duty in Moscow, Russia, during the cold war, and rose to the rank of Navy Captain. John and his lovely wife are still our friends after all these years. He is another of my unsung heroes.

Friday Nights

Friday nights at OCS always included two activities. First there was "sports night." The entire officer candidate population participated with all companies competing against each other. Each company had a football team, a basketball team, wrestlers, a swim team, dead man carry team, and other sports. The competitions were sometimes rough, because there was a reward for the company that accumulated the most points during sports night. So rough, in fact, that we had some injuries, including one of our guys who broke his leg playing football. Because of his injuries, he had to "roll back" to a class coming through behind us in order to make up the class work he missed.

We had a college swimmer in our company, so he generally took the bulk of the swimming assignment. But I would also swim occasionally if we were short of swimmers. I was assigned a different sport. For some strange reason, as scrawny as I was, I was assigned to the dead man carry competition. In this event, participants had to carry a classmate on their backs over a course, while running as fast as they could. My partner in the competition was my classmate, Bob, who I sometimes called "Pasqui" (pass key), a mangling of his last name. After I had completed the course carrying Bob, he would then hoist me on his back, and complete the same course in reverse. Amazingly, Echo Company usually finished in the top three of all the teams, giving us an excellent point-count in the Friday night competitions.

Officer candidates came from all over the nation, and most of them had not been athletes at their respective colleges. So in each company, there were maybe only one or two guys who had participated in college athletics. Hence, choosing individuals to participate in each event was hit or miss. Some would do well in their events, and others would give it their all, but not necessarily excel. We must have had a fairly well balanced physical group, because our company excelled at sports night and won the competition almost every week. As the winners, we were presented with a ribbon that was attached to our guide-on pole. So during the following week while marching to our activities, other companies could see that we were the head jocks on campus. Whoopee. That ribbon was not the real incentive for winning the sports night competition.

After a week of classes and the conclusion of Friday sports night, all companies held an intense "field day" to clean their respective living areas—hallways, heads (Navy talk for bathrooms and showers), and individual rooms. All of this cleaning was in preparation for a Saturday morning, white glove inspection by an officer and recorder. Three things could happen as a result of this inspection. If the entire company failed the inspection, the company would not be eligible for weekend liberty and would be forced to undergo remedial marching or physical training. If an individual dorm room failed, the two occupants would face the same treatment. If the entire company passed inspection, liberty would commence for the whole company following the inspection lasting until Sunday evening. No one wanted to fail that inspection, so late Friday night, all company members were down on their hands and knees with scrubbing equipment to make the company area shine. To me, inspections were a necessary evil and a pain in the rear end. But, happily, if a company won the Friday night sports event, that company was exempt from standing Saturday morning inspection. If you did not have to stand Saturday morning inspection, you could begin liberty while the rest of the companies stayed behind for inspection. That was the payoff for winning sports night.

There was another way to bypass Saturday inspections. Every Saturday morning after a week of classes, and before the Saturday inspection was held, all of the companies participated in a "pass in review." All companies would line up in formation, and then march into one door of the gymnasium, circle around the floor, and proceed out the door. Inside the gymnasium were the Navy Captain, Commanding Officer of OCS, and his staff. They were there to grade each company on its marching prowess, and the winning company of the pass in review was also exempt from the subsequent inspection. As I said, our company was skilled at marching, and most of the time we won the pass in review. If Echo Company won both sports night and pass in review, we were denying another company the opportunity to be exempt from Saturday inspection. Hence, there was always a bit of "rivalry" from the other companies to knock us off our perch. And even though we were often closely challenged on Friday nights, we usually prevailed.

I recall one Saturday morning that was not the usual routine. I had been informed the day before that I was to report to medical sick bay on Saturday morning before the pass in review. I did not know what this was about, but I reported as ordered. A Navy doctor then saw me and told me that they needed an x-ray of my kidneys. During my sophomore year of college, I had been hospitalized with kidney stones. The Navy wanted to make sure I was clear of the malady, and there was no chance that I would require hospitalization later for another bout of kidney stones. Now bear in mind that I had taken a rather lengthy physical to be accepted to OCS in the first place, and there was no indication of trouble at that time. But the doctor insisted, and he gave me two little pills to take and told me to come back after lunch for the x-ray. I took the pills and returned to the barracks to prepare for pass in review. The doctor did not tell me what the pills were for, so I thought nothing more about it. UNTIL—we were standing in formation waiting for our turn to enter the gym, and my innards started rumbling and aching. My stomach ached, and primal noises were now emanating from the lower nether of my body. Suddenly, it became clear that I would need to visit a head and soon. Well, you get the idea. But we were moving forward, ready to enter the gym for our pass in review. I could not leave formation and so proceeded to tighten every muscle, and I mean every muscle I could, struggling to march in pass in review. Oh, I was in complete agony. Those two little pills must have been dynamite pills, because my innards were about to blow up. I was later told that they were very efficient at cleaning the entire bowel so that a good x-ray could be taken. Oh, great! Ever so slowly and painfully, it seemed, we marched around the gym. It seemed like hours, and I was gritting my teeth so hard that my jaw ached, as well as other muscles. We finally reached the doors of the gym and went outdoors. I threw the guide-on pole to a surprised John and took off running for the barracks as fast as my poor fatigued and over-worked sphincter would allow. Would I or wouldn't I make it? I hit the doors of the barracks and stumbled into the nearest head. Hey, the tension was killing me, too. But, yes, I thankfully made it, but with no time to spare. Later that afternoon, I reported to the clinic for the x-ray, and sure enough, there was no problem. But that was one of the very few pass in reviews that we did not win. I think it had something to do with the guide-on trying to hurry the marching cadence, or something like that. Thank you, Doctor.

Roomie

Following hell week, we were able to choose our roommates. Nimitz Hall, our barracks, was set up in wings with a company in each wing. The wings had several two person rooms, and the wing residents shared a community head with toilets and showers. My roommate turned out to be Tom, from Montevideo, Minnesota. Tom and I got along great. He and I thought alike and laughed at the same things, but he was quicker to pick up some of the more technical courses and could help me where I was weak. I struggled with ship tactics and navigation, and Tom counseled me in these courses. Tom had brought his car with him from Minnesota. He had a nifty 1957 Chevrolet Belair four-door sedan with a little 283 V-8. We put a lot of miles on that car during our weekend liberties, and it only failed us once when the weather was so cold that it would not start. I'll bet Tom wishes he had that car today.

As I recall, after graduation from OCS Tom was assigned to a destroyer out of Long Beach, but deployed out of Japan, and while on active duty, he met and married a Navy nurse. They still live in Minnesota. I spoke with him by telephone recently, and his personality is still the same. Tom is one of the nicest, most honest, and upright guys I met in the military—another unsung hero.

In any military training environment, young men and women come from all across the nation and are thrown into a completely strange, new living situation. Each recruit is a unique individual, and believe me, many of them have some strange quirks. Take for instance Cort House, who was actually in a neighboring company—not an Echo Company member. Cort's mom and dad must have sat down and began thinking about baby names. Somebody must have said they thought Cort would be a great name, since he was already a House.

Every morning before classes started there would be a personnel inspection and room inspection. One of the things the upper classmen loved to do was to come in and look at each bunk to make sure that it was made to Navy standards and made up so tightly that a quarter would bounce when it was dropped on the made-up bunk. Well, apparently old Cort House was not doing so well in making up his bunk and kept failing the inspection. Finally, after a few days he got it right, but he was so tired of getting yelled at for his poor bunk preparation, that once he got it right, he figured out a way to never fail the inspection again. He simply began sleeping on the floor under his bunk, using a couple of towels and blankets for bedding. But he must not have been getting a very good night's sleep under the bunk, because he really started to look physically exhausted. So one day, a member of our company asked a member of Cort's company what was wrong with Cort as he looked so bad. The response was that Cort was sleeping on the floor under his bunk so he would not have to make up the bunk every morning. We all roared at that. Shortly thereafter, while Cort's company was out of the building, Cort's perfect bunk was mysteriously torn apart with the sheets and blankets left on the floor. No more cheating for him. From then on, he would need to make up his bunk every day like the rest of us. No one ever discovered who the perpetrator of that incident was… Hmmm.

Now I am not saying old Cort was crazy or anything, but here are a couple of other incidents. One cold day, we were wearing our pea coats and gloves because of the temperature. When we reached our classrooms, we would remove our coats, hats, and gloves. As we were sitting through a lecture in class this particular morning, John happened to look over at Cort, who was also in the class. Cort had his gloves in his lap, and would take a glove and blow into it and then hold the glove closed, keeping the air trapped inside it. Then, using his other hand, he would shake hands with the inflated glove. He did this over and over again. The instructor did not seem to notice, but it was all the rest of us could do to stifle a laugh.

In another incident, one day John needed to meet the company commander of the neighboring company, of which Cort was a member. In each dorm room, there were two, six-foot tall steel lockers in which each officer candidate kept his clothing and personal belongings. As John entered the room of that company commander, who incidentally shared his room with Cort, he was immediately taken aback. There, perched on top of one of those tall, steel lockers was Cort House. He was in a crouched position, with his arms folded, and his elbows out at a right angle to his body. He rotated his head from left to right, continuously surveying the room. Depending upon your perspective, he appeared to be either an eagle, or a gargoyle. John was shocked at this scene, but conducted his business with the other company commander, who seemed oblivious to the watchful presence above. John returned to Echo Company and related the experience. We all agreed that old Cort, "was a very strange guy."

White Balls

Although it was Navy slang, I have no idea where the term "white ball" originated and have been unable to track it down in research. But at

OCS, a white ball, or white ball duty, was defined as being assigned to an easy task instead of a more tedious or "male bovine excrement" task. Example—if one sailor is assigned to a ditch digging detail and another sailor is assigned to drive an officer's car, the driver obviously has the white ball detail. And if he has that detail, he is "riding the white ball express."

Every morning after getting up, getting dressed, and marching to breakfast, we returned to our rooms to be sure everything was ship shape and ready for an inspection. Everyone stood outside his room, and as the inspectors came around to each room, the two OC's who occupied the room would announce to the inspectors that the room was ready for inspection. You would then follow the inspector into the room and watch as he tore into everything and ran his white gloves over all surfaces. What a pain in the keester! With my wise-ass attitude, I did not see any great value in that nonsense, and I kept my eyes and ears open for a short cut.

Lo and behold, my roommate Tom and I learned that there was a call out for officer candidates to sing in the OCS choir. Tom and I huddled and soon found that we had both sung in choirs in our civilian lives. We inquired about the location of the try-outs and hot-footed it over to participate. We discovered that the primary reason for the choir was to sing at the base chapel every Sunday morning. We tried out, and both of us were appointed to the choir. The best part of being in the choir was that the choir held rehearsals every morning, after breakfast and before the first class of the day. That was also when morning inspections were held. Tom and I had just secured a huge white ball duty. We were excused from all morning inspections after that. We were riding the white ball express!

Our OCS class timing was such that we spanned the Christmas holidays. Therefore, another assignment of the choir was to sing a Christmas concert for all the officer candidates and all active duty officers. Apparently, attendance at the concert was a "command performance." In the Navy, a command performance means that everyone in the command's wardroom (all officers attached to the command) is required to attend. The concert was held in the gymnasium, and it was completely filled with attendees. I was asked to sing a solo section in one of the numbers for the performance, and with a packed house, I was nervous. As the concert started, I looked out and there in the front row was the Navy Captain CO of the school with his wife sitting next to him. Sitting next to them was the Navy Commander XO of the school and his wife. It was another one of those, oh crap (or something to that effect) moments. I did not need them to be sitting right in front to add to my jitters. Just before I started to sing my solo part, I looked to see the CO's wife looking down with a scowl on her face. With that less than encouraging sign, I was even more concerned. I started my solo, and as I sang I was able to glance at the CO and his wife. Both were staring at me, and my stomach twisted some more. But then, suddenly the CO's wife started smiling at me, and I knew it was going to be all right. We finished the concert, and she and the CO came and shook hands with the choir members and extended their best wishes to everyone. Christmas was going to be good that year.

The school had a mandatory close-down through the Christmas holidays, and we were given two weeks of leave. Tom and I jumped into his Chevy and drove to the Boston airport. We boarded planes and headed home for Christmas. He caught a flight to Minneapolis, and I caught one to Des Moines. Janet was there to meet me, and we had a great holiday with both of our parents. At the end of the two weeks, we headed back to OCS for the final month and a half of training.

Chief Rudy

The physical training instructor was drilling a group of Officer Candidates. "I want every man to lie on his back, put his legs in the air and move them as though you were riding a bicycle," he explained. "Now begin!" After a few minutes, one of the men stopped. "Why did you stop, Smith?" demanded the instructor. "If you please, sir," said Smith, "I'm coasting downhill for a while."

—*Author unknown*

Do you remember the scene in the movie "Officer and a Gentleman" where the Officer Candidate, Richard Gere, was in physical training class and the instructor, Lou Gossett, really worked him over? Of course you do. I decided that our Chief Rudy may have been the inspiration for Gossett's character. Echo Company had reported to our first physical training class in the gymnasium, and we sat down on the floor. Waiting for us was a black instructor standing up on the stage in the gym. He began talking to us, and he said something like this.

"My name is Chief Rudy. I will be your physical training instructor while you are here at Officer Candidate School." He continued, "This is my gymnasium, and while you are in here with me, I will be your poppa, your momma, and your worst friend. I will kick your asses around this gym so much that you will be hollering for your real momma. Well, she ain't here, and I am. And you will do everything I say at double time, or you do it all again 'til I'm happy. Are there any questions?"

I think one dumb clod raised his hand.

At that, Chief Rudy said, "I don't want any of your momma's boy dumb ass questions. Now get up off your asses and stand at attention." Chief Rudy then whipped off his warm up sweats and stripped down to his shorts and tennis shoes. We stood and looked at him in awe. The man was one big walking muscle. He had the arms of a weight lifter, and the abs of someone inhuman. We instantly knew that we were in big trouble.

After we were all standing at attention, he then said, "And now we are going to run. Start moving, move, move, move!"

And we all began running. Chief Rudy opened the gym doors, and we started running down the road, away from the gym. And we ran, and we kept running until all of us were gasping and in pain. Three or four of us had lost our breakfasts along the way. We then turned around and ran back to the gym.

After we were all inside, Chief Rudy said, "Now I want to see push-ups. Move, move, move." And we started doing push-ups.

We did as many as we could, and the Chief then said, "Roll over, we're going to do some sit ups."

And we started sit-ups. Again, we did as many as we could. At least two guys had rushed for the door and regurgitated whatever breakfast they may have still had available. We were all in pain. Thankfully, the class ended, and we returned to the barracks to clean up and head to our other classes. Throughout the day, the primary topic of discussion among us was Chief Rudy, and whether or not he was trying to legally kill us. The consensus was that he must be criminally insane. Of course, other much more colorful phraseology was used to describe Chief Rudy. He had us right where he wanted us.

For at least the first month, every day with Chief Rudy was just as described. Of course, as time passed, the inevitable happened. Guys started losing some of the excess weight they had been carrying, and we all became stronger. We could all run without getting sick and complete our calisthenics without gasping. Chief Rudy kept after us, and he did all of the exercising right along with us. When we left OCS, we were probably in the best physical condition that any of us had ever been. The marching and the sports nights helped, but Chief Rudy is the one who got us into shape. As much as we may have hated the initial indoctrination into our physical conditioning, we all formed a great admiration for that mean little unsung hero, Chief Rudy.

Lieutenant Clang

Our ship tactics instructor was Lieutenant Clang. For some reason, I could not get a good reading on this guy. One day he would come in to class all cheerful and want to be your buddy, and other days he would come in and be the most pompous, arrogant lieutenant you would ever meet. Ship tactics was a hard course for me. It dealt with the use of ship directions, speeds, and other variables to determine the best plan for ship's actions, and for avoiding another ship. It included learning various ship-to-ship signals in codes that were retrieved from Navy operations books. For a great deal of the course, I struggled. But during the last quarter of the course, it all became clearer, and I began to understand the problems and devise solutions. Lt. Clang never really warmed up to any of us. He was there to teach a course, and it was his opinion that we were all so inferior to him that he simply tolerated us. So we all tried to remain on his good side, not ask any stupid questions in class, and humor him with whatever he wanted to know.

One day in class, Lt. Clang used the term "nooner," a Navy term that I learned the hard way. (Actually I have found in my life that I learn almost everything the hard way.) Lt. Clang entered the class room a few minutes late. On this day, the class was right after lunch.

He started blathering, and then said something to the effect, "I was late because I had to have a nooner."

Now remember, this is a room full of twenty-two or twenty-three year old young men in peak physical condition. Naturally, a nooner could be any number of things. But my sorry excuse for a brain suddenly conjured up a colorful mental picture of Lt. Clang hustling home at lunch time and being "romantically involved" with his significant other. With that image in mind and thinking that he was making a somewhat ribald joke, I burst out laughing. But egad, I was the only guy in the classroom laughing. Next, I heard these words, "Mr. Duermeyer!" (The phrase, "Mr. Duermeyer!" will appear in other parts of my writing, and in almost all cases it will be preceded or followed by an explanation of why I was in trouble again. I became afraid to hear someone call my name.)

Lt. Clang continued, "What is so funny?"

I was stuck for words. Lt. Clang knew he had me, and he was enjoying every second I was on the hot seat. I managed to stumble and mumble something, and Lt. Clang chewed on me a little more before class proceeded. One or two of my classmates seemed to know what a nooner was, and after class they explained that a nooner was a short *nap* right after lunch. Geez Jim, way to go. But if the truth were known, I think I made Lt. Clang's day. After all, a Lieutenant has to have his fun too, even if it is at my expense.

Later in my Navy career I also learned that the term "nooner" does indeed have other meanings. 'Nuff said.

Senior Chief Drawl

One of the courses taught at OCS was seamanship. The course taught us greenhorn OCs some of the nuts and bolts (literally and figuratively) of the deck machinery commonly used onboard ships. Such things as rope (called line in the Navy), cable (called wire in the Navy), pulleys (called blocks in the Navy), anchors and their corresponding chains (called ground tackle by the Navy), and hundreds of other terms all of which became part of our vocabulary in preparation for Navy Officer duty. Because I am a bit of a gear head, I like machinery and knowing how it works and runs. So I really enjoyed the seamanship course. It was very mechanical, with lots of new and different kinds of machinery.

Our Senior Chief Instructor was a bit of a character. He was a senior chief boatswain's mate, so he knew his way around the deck machinery of a ship. He had a real ruddy complexion, which led us to believe he probably knew his way around the liberty port taverns too. But he wore a gold crow (navy petty officer insignia) and had an armful of gold chevrons-one for every four years of Navy service. As a chief, a gold crow and gold chevrons are worn only if your behavior, performance, and deportment have been historically good. Senior Chief Drawl apparently had stayed out of trouble during his career. OCS instructor duty at that time was usually only granted to top quality enlisted men and officers.

The senior chief had an odd voice. He sounded like his mouth was full of marbles, and he talked in a slow southern drawl. So sometimes, we could not quite understand him when he threw a new Navy term at us. But he was well liked by our class.

As in most Navy instruction, an instructor will try to emphasize a term or idea that might appear in a later exam on the subject. When Senior Chief would run across one of these "special" terms, he repeated the term or idea, and then kicked his podium. This meant that you had better be listening, because the term would probably appear in a subsequent test. He would teach the term, and then, crash, crash, kick the podium.

One day, he was talking about pelican hooks. A pelican hook is a special kind of steel clamp that is hinged and can be used in various situations. A specific example would be to clamp onto an anchor chain to keep it secure on the deck of a ship. The Senior Chief kept kicking the podium. We could not figure out why he <u>kept</u> doing that, so, one of us asked for clarification.

The Senior Chief responded, "Look, when you take the test, and you see a question of which you are in doubt, the answer is pelican hook."

Well, that seemed odd, but sure enough, in that week's seamanship test, there were a couple ambiguous questions. But remembering what the senior chief had said, we answered them, pelican hook. Sure enough, the correct answers were pelican hook. There were at least five test questions having the answer of "pelican hook." From then on, when any of us were discussing ANY topic and there was a question, or when we were just talking among ourselves, and because it just sounded silly, we would all say, "When in doubt, pelican hook!" Yes, the opportunities for humor at OCS were fleeting and rare.

USS Buttercup

Another part of our seamanship training had to do with maintaining a ship's water-tight integrity and making minor emergency repairs to the ship's piping or temporary emergency repairs for hull damage. We learned how to slow or stop water from entering the ship from damage incurred in an emergency, such as battle damage or machinery breakdown. In the classroom and in films, we watched the use of various pipe patches, wooden plugs, and even the use of mattresses to block the flow of water into a ship. But, the Navy has a way to simulate these happenings in a controlled classroom environment. Well, not exactly a classroom. Imagine a water-tight steel room, with steel walls, steel floor, steel ceiling, with glass windows on one side. Running through this room are a large number of pipes. There are steel decking plates on the floor and electric lights on the ceiling. Now imagine being in this room; the room is flooding, there is no way out, and all of the lights go off. You need to fix and patch the leaks before the room is completely flooded. Doesn't that sound like a fun game? I can tell you from firsthand experience, it is not fun! It is damage control training in the ship simulator known as USS Buttercup.

The day came for our company's Buttercup training. We were told to bring an extra set of uniform clothing on that class day, but not why. When we arrived at the simulator, we removed our shoes and pulled on rubber boots. We were told that there were flashlights, patches, tools, and everything needed to patch the holes in the simulator. We then all entered the Buttercup. As we apprehensively stood in the simulator, we could see the instructors outside the glass wall. They were there to observe us.

Suddenly, one of the pipes began spewing water, and we scrambled to find the proper size patch to repair this pipe. As we made some progress, another pipe burst, and then another. We were scrambling frantically, desperately trying to stay ahead of the frigid incoming water. This exercise took place in the winter, and the water that was being pumped into the compartment must have been forty degrees. It was numbingly cold. We were not told this, but I believe the water may have been pumped directly from Narragansett Bay, it was that cold.

Next, one of the steel walls erupted and water poured into the room. The water kept rising, and soon, we were waist deep in ice water, trying to fix leaks that had virtually sprung from every pipe in the room, and from the gaping hole in the wall. And then, all of the lights went out, even outside the glass wall. We were now in a room with water rushing into it, in the dark, with only flashlights to help us find the sources of the incoming water. When the water reached chest height, the lights came on, and the instructors shouted to us on an intercom that our beloved Buttercup had sunk. Exercise over. And the water began to drain out of the simulator.

We stood there freezing, shaking, and feeling rather embarrassed that we had not made a better showing. But we did not dwell on this too much, because after the water was drained from the simulator, the instructors said we would now repeat the exercise. Oh, no, here we go again. A pipe burst, then another, and so on as we valiantly struggled to patch some of the leaks. Result—old Buttercup went to Davy Jones locker again.

Once more, the simulator was quickly drained, and by this time, we all were purple from the cold. Our hands and fingers hurt like crazy, and we had difficulty moving our fingers. Then the intercom blared, "Stand by," and the water began again. For what seemed like a very long time, we struggled, again trying to make the patches hold back the flooding. We could usually properly attach a few of them, but the water flow was far too heavy to ever get ahead. Finally, the flow of water diminished and then stopped. The instructors had turned off the flow. Our day in the USS Buttercup was over.

There were hot showers in the simulator building, and warm water never felt so good. Later, our instructors told us that no one ever keeps the Buttercup afloat. That activity was designed to illustrate to officer candidates the steps required for, and the difficulty of, damage repair in a real life, crisis situation. Our frozen extremities attested to the fact that they had made their point.

Learning about fire fighting was another damage control exercise that we experienced. Imagine again, a steel room, really a very large box, with steel on all four sides, the deck, and overhead. The doors into and out of the box are steel ship doors, with dogging levers to open and close them. Now imagine this whole room on fire, and you will need to enter the room and put out the fire.

Our large group was divided into smaller fire fighting teams. Each team would take a turn and enter the building to extinguish the fire. In this exercise, the steel building had ship's fuel oil spread on top of the water in the bottom of the room, and there were catwalk grates just above the water and oil. There were no interior lights.

When the instructors were ready, the fuel oil was ignited, and black smoke began billowing from all openings in the steel box. The student team, dragging fire fighting gear with them, opened the door and entered the building to attempt to extinguish the fire. The fuel oil fire must be extinguished with a special foam agent being sprayed at the base of the fire to eventually smother the fire by depriving it of oxygen. In addition, a water hose is also brought in to knock down the flames and provide a cooling effect for the firefighters.

On the scheduled day, our company and one other company reported together for the fire fighting drill. We all donned heavy rain gear, boots, and helmets. We then entered the building with an instructor at our shoulder to guide us and teach us how to attack the fire. There were at least two students who could not enter the building. They were just plain terrified of the fiery, smoky, claustrophobic situation. Once inside, we could see nothing in the dense, black smoke. The fire was roaring from somewhere, and we were enveloped in complete blackness. We struggled to breathe with the thick black soot suspended in the smoke. The instructor shouted at us to look for the light of the flames, and if we looked down, we could see glimpses of orange flames through the smoke. That was where the fire had to be attacked; at the base of the flames. While the water hose sprayed above us, we used our foam sprayers, aiming them at the base of the flames. After a time, the fire subsided and was soon out.

Being in that confined, burning space was a terrifying experience, but it served to make us very aware that things can go horribly wrong on board a ship, and that danger from a horrific fire is always with you while shipboard.

Navigation

The Navigator—The destroyer escort with the ensign navigator was steaming along and the ensign sent a surreptitious signal light message to the lighthouse they were passing. It read, did I pass your lighthouse three days ago? The light house responded that they had indeed passed here going the opposite direction three days ago. The ensign then self-importantly reported

to the ship's captain, "Good news Skipper, I've plotted our
course and we are right on track to return to port."
—*Author unknown*

Of all the courses at OCS, I struggled with navigation more than any other. At that time, all navigators on Navy ships used celestial navigation, and Long Range Radio Navigation (LORAN). GPS was not yet in use. At OCS we were taught line-of-sight, dead reckoning, radar, and celestial navigation. With celestial navigation, just like mariners of old, a sextant was used by a navigator to measure, in degrees, the height from the horizon of stars and/or the sun. For example, after properly adjusting the settings on the sextant and synchronizing the time with the atomic clock in Colorado via radio, a star could be observed through the sextant, and the angle from the horizon to the star could be determined in degrees above the horizon. In addition, the sighting was made and synchronized with a stop watch to record the exact time of the sighting. By using this measured angle, a series of Navy navigation publications would be consulted to obtain other figures, and after working a series of mathematical processes and filling in the blanks on a special navigation sight form, the result would be a number from which a line could be drawn on a plotting chart to represent that number. Reading several stars in this fashion would provide intersecting lines on the plotting chart, and where those lines met and crossed would determine the location of the ship at that time. Using almost the same principles, shooting the sun at a specific time of the day (called local apparent noon) would give the navigator his latitude at that instant in time.

If this all sounds easy enough, for a dunderhead like me it was rocket science. Most of this entire process is simply a matter of learning the correct sequence of the steps, and just as importantly, knowing which Navy publication to consult to get the sequential figures. Finally, there were the mathematical processes to be performed. Now, for a social science/business major like me, this was all too much, and I had difficulty in getting all of the steps in sequence to arrive at the correct answers. To this day, I wonder if the Navy may have needed officers so badly at the time that they let me slip through this course. But wait, there is real irony here. The Navy would later, in its all-knowing wisdom, order me to become the navigator on a ship using only celestial navigation. We will explore that later.

Bob and the Tower
In addition to passing the academic curriculum at OCS, each student was required to pass physical training, which included a swimming compo-

nent. Each candidate must meet two requirements: first, to swim a minimum of 50 yards; and second, jump from a thirty foot tower into the pool. The thinking behind this was to simulate jumping off the deck of a sinking ship. Sinking ship? I didn't think I had signed up to be on any sinking ship.

I mentioned my friend Bob (Pasqui) earlier. He was a great guy, an Italian from upstate New York. He and I were a strong team at Friday night sports night. Anyway, the day came for our swimming test and the tower jump. One by one, Echo Company members climbed the ladder to the top of the tower, peered over the edge, and jumped to the pool below. I had completed my jump and was waiting at the edge of the pool for the swimming test to begin. I was watching the tower.

Soon, it was Bob's turn to jump off the tower. He very slowly climbed the ladder, and after a time, he reached the top of the tower. He stood there for a moment until the instructor yelled at him to jump. Bob slowly moved to the front edge of the tower. It then occurred to me that he was scared to death. I just knew he was not going to make that jump. He stood there literally shaking and was frozen in place. The instructor kept yelling at him to jump, but there was no response. The instructor then went over to the tower and started climbing up to the top. When he got to the top he again started "verbally coaxing" Bob to jump. Bob was frozen and would not move. Finally the instructor saw the futility of his effort, and told Bob to climb down the ladder, which he did.

In front of the class, the instructor berated and ridiculed Bob for not completing the jump. This instructor finally asked Bob why he had not jumped—as simple as that. Bob responded, "I, I, I, can't swim, sir." Holy mackerel! A Navy officer candidate who couldn't swim! This seemed really strange to me. Why would a person enter Navy OCS and not know how to swim? In addition, I couldn't remember meeting anyone of adult age who didn't know how to swim, since swimming had been a big part of my growing up.

The instructor then stated to the entire class that we would now take the swimming test, and he asked Bob if he could do the test. Bob told him no. The swim test was to swim 50 yards, or two lengths of the OCS pool. The swimmers varied in their swimming skill, but all of the class completed the swim, except Bob. After the rest of the class completed the swim test, the instructor made a point of reiterating to the class that anyone who could not pass the tower jump and swim test would not pass OCS. Yikes. My buddy Bob might fail OCS just because of a stupid swim test. Then the instructor addressed the class again. He said that it was the responsibility of the class to make sure one of their classmates did not fail this swim test. He asked for volunteers to work with Bob to help him complete the test. Contrary to the military code that says, 'never volunteer for anything,' I raised my hand. The instructor said, "All right, it is your responsibility to get this guy through the test."

Every Saturday afternoon for the next six weeks, Bob and I went to the pool for swimming lessons. I was a certified Water Safety Instructor and had taught swimming for years while in high school and college, so I thought this would be a piece of cake. I had always taught young, malleable kids how to swim. Now, I had this hard-headed adult from New York to teach. It just wasn't the same. Bob's fears were already ingrained. We worked and struggled every Saturday afternoon.

I finally said, "Pasqui, I'm going to teach you to dog paddle if it kills me."

We kept at it, and we finally did it. He got the rudiments of dog paddling, and he could go at least one length of the pool. We needed two lengths, let alone addressing the tower issue. More work, more Saturdays. Bob finally got to the point that he could do the two laps, and we knew what was coming next. The following Saturday, we arrived at the pool, and I told him that I was going up the tower and he needed to follow right behind me. He did it. I took him to the edge of the tower, and I sat down on the edge and told him to sit with me. He did.

I said, "See, if you sit here, it doesn't look like it is as far down there."

I'm not sure he bought that, but we continued to sit there for a while, and we discussed the fact that God gave both of us certain talents. I happened to be pretty good at swimming, but struggled in some of the class work. On the other hand, he struggled at swimming but excelled in the class room. So, I was here to make sure that his struggle did not result in him washing out of OCS. But I could not force him. He would have to make the jump himself. Then I told him to keep his seat and watch me. I stood up and jumped into the pool. When I rose to the surface, I told Bob he had to do the same thing. I couldn't do it for him. He stood up.

Then I told him, "Pasqui, I am going to stay right here in the water, waiting on you to jump. And when you jump, if I have to, I will pull you up to the surface where you can swim. I won't let you get hurt or drown, but I can't tread water here forever, so let's get this done!"

Bob stood up on that tower for a long time, while I was treading water down below. I thought this was going to end the same way as it had a few weeks ago. But suddenly, Bob jumped. He hit the water near me, and I dove down to watch him. He struggled to the surface and panicked. I figured this was coming, so I grabbed his upper arm and yelled at him to swim. He fought a bit more but then settled into his dog paddle rhythm, and I guided him over to the side. We did three more jumps that day, and he was able to surface, recover, and swim to the side. Success.

The following Saturday, we met the swimming instructor at the pool, with my roommate Tom there to watch. It was rather anticlimactic, as Bob did his 50 yard dog paddle and then jumped off the tower.

The instructor congratulated both of us, but pulled me aside later to ask, "How did you ever get that 'fraidy cat' off the tower."

I said, "It wasn't me who did it. Bob did it himself. He just needed a little encouragement."

After that, the three of us headed to town and celebrated. As we toasted Bob's success, I knew I had gained a friend for life, and I was happy. It is not always the big, newsworthy actions that make a difference in a person's life. Sometimes it is the small, personal conquests. Bob, who had overcome his fears in order to continue his military career, is one of my unsung heroes.

Jan and I were pleasantly surprised during our 1969 Charleston tour to find out that Bob was also in Charleston, and also assigned to an MSO, the USS Valor (MSO-472). We were able to get together a few times with him and his fiancé during that time.

I called Bob at his home in New York recently, and he is still the same great guy I knew at OCS.

Liberty Call, Newport, R.I.
My roommate and best buddy Tom and I spent almost every weekend together on liberty. Because we did not have to stand Saturday morning inspection, he and I were able to leave the base about noon. We would then go to a restaurant to enjoy a better meal than the usual OCS fare. A steak or sea food and a couple beers were a real treat. After lunch, we usually went to the Viscount Hotel basement. Every Saturday, they had a bar set up with a local rock and roll band playing. Almost every officer candidate from the base went there. Besides the band and bar, the draw was that there was a girls' college in Newport, and every Saturday the girls from that school would also come to the Viscount Hotel. Girls from a nearby nursing school would drop in too. We had fun, and I was certain several times that Tom was going to end up engaged to one of those girls. But, he stayed the course, remained single, and we kept out of trouble.

One of the other places we frequented in Newport was a smoky old bar, called Hurley's. Hurley's was operated, staffed, and frequented by African-Americans. They had an all-black combo of musicians playing Saturday afternoons and evenings. They played rock and roll, R&B, and jazz. We really liked that place for the music and would sit at the bar almost directly in front of the band, which was up on a little elevated stage.

One afternoon, they were playing Otis Redding's, "Sitting on the Dock of the Bay." When it came to the part of the song that is a whistling solo, a guy in the band shoved the microphone in front of me. Well, I may have had a couple beers, but I could still whistle, and I whistled that part so well that all the other OCs in the bar burst out cheering. Oh, oh. I was in trouble. Most of them knew I sang in the OCS choir, so they started chanting that I should get up and sing. They were ribbing me and trying to embarrass me. What they didn't know was that I sang in a rock band in college at Iowa, so I was not a stranger to a microphone. I sure did not know how this was going to turn out, but I jumped off the barstool and climbed up on the stage. So there I was; with my white boy face in a funny Navy uniform, surrounded by the black musicians and an audience that was half black. Oh, boy. I conspired for a moment with the lead guitar player, and he did a little "wood shedding" for a couple minutes to figure out a proper key, and said, "OK." I then started in with a little Ray Charles, "What'd I say," and cranked it up. Soon, the whole place was jumping, and the audience was singing along in the repeat sections. The guys and gals in the audience paired up and were dancing all around the room. That was fun. Next, the band and I jumped on the Animals song, "House of The Rising Sun." We concluded with that, and I climbed down off the stage. The guys were hooting and hollering, and we all had a great time. Tom and I managed to get to Hurley's several Saturday evenings, and sometimes I sang those same two songs with all my rowdy OC buddies. Add "Smoky Bar Club Singer" to my resume.

On Saturday evenings we usually went to the Navy Officer's Club on the base for some really great chow. Then, we would head back to town to another bar we might know, and finally, head back to base. Sunday mornings, Tom and I attended chapel and sang in the choir. Sunday noon, we would be back to the Officer's Club for a good lunch, and then either watch a football game in the barracks or go to a sports bar to watch a game and have a beer. Sunday night was back to the books for classes on Monday. Weekends were not all that exciting, but they sure beat the monotony of the class week.

Graduation

Graduation from Navy Officer Candidate School was February 14, 1969. I know that date well, because Janet and I were to be married on the 22nd of February. It was also one week after my twenty-third birthday.

Effective on that Valentine's Day, we were commissioned officers in the U.S. Navy. It is a Navy tradition that the brand new ensign must give a dollar to the first enlisted man who salutes him. After we received our certificates of commissioning and left the gymnasium in our Navy officer uniforms, each with one bright gold stripe on our sleeves, we passed one of the instructor chiefs who had set up camp outside the door, saluting all of the new ensigns as they exited the building. That guy must have made $500 that day.

We had all received our official orders and were being sent to the fleet to become the new, green ensign on board our respective ships. I was to go to an ocean going minesweeper in Charleston, South Carolina, the USS Rival (MSO-468). Tom was heading for a destroyer out of Long Beach, presently deployed in Yokosuka, Japan, and John was to report to the USS Hissem (DER-400), at Pearl Harbor.

The Wedding

I flew home to Iowa the day after graduation to help Janet prepare for our wedding if I could. We were to be married in Emmetsburg, Iowa, where her parents lived. On the 21st, it began to snow, with a real white-out blizzard. It snowed all day and night. Nearly three feet of snow fell, but with the stormy high winds there were drifts of fifteen feet deep. The snow had drifted as high as the eaves of her parent's house, and because of the weight of the snow, on the morning of our wedding; I was on the roof of her parents' house shoveling snow off the roof. We were afraid the roof would collapse, which had happened to a couple of other houses in the area. Another concern was whether or not guests would be able to travel to the wedding because of the treacherous road conditions. But upper Midwest spirit prevailed, and all of the wedding party and many of the out-of-town invited guests arrived as scheduled.

The wedding went off without a hitch, and after the ceremony and reception, we changed clothes and started driving in the precarious snowy road conditions to Minneapolis for our honeymoon. It had been a killer of a day, and we were both out on our feet. We were both so tired, in fact, that when we got up next morning in the Minneapolis hotel to go to breakfast, we could not find our suitcases. After much head scratching, I sheepishly opened the door to our room and saw the suitcases sitting in the hallway. I was so tired the night before that I had left them in the hall outside the room. No problem, everybody knows that newlyweds don't need suitcases!

After a few days, we headed to Charleston, South Carolina, where I would join my first ship in my Navy career. Janet had graduated from college in three years (smarty pants), and she had been teaching school in Minneapolis for a year while I finished college and OCS. She had a car, a 1962 Mercury Meteor, brown and white in color. And because it was brown in color, and a bit sleek, we affectionately called it the "Tapered T _ _ d," or TT for short. TT was a good little car and got us easily to Charleston. Don't all newlyweds remember their first car?

We arrived in Charleston and began looking for an apartment. One of the places we identified in the newspaper was close to the Navy base, so we called the contact number. I asked if they still had the vacancy advertised in the paper. The man's response was that he was not sure and he would have to meet us at the apartment house to check his books to be sure the apartment was not already rented. Later, the landlord showed up and introduced himself. He then said that his purpose in meeting us at the apartment building was so make sure that we were the right color. Right color? Coming from the upper Midwest in those days, where there were almost no people of color, this was a real shock to us. Our experiences had just been broadened as we witnessed lingering southern housing discrimination. Later, we moved from that apartment to half of a duplex conveniently located near the school where Janet had secured a teaching position. It was a small two bedroom concrete block duplex, and the rent was $100/mo. I told the landlord that I would mow the lawn if he would lower the rent to $75, and he agreed. What a deal! We did some fix up work on the duplex, and it was a great little place for us.

Jan and I had a German Shepherd puppy named Heidi. She was a sweet dog, and we loved her dearly, but she had one annoying habit. She was a digger; and not just small holes. She would dig moon craters! One day, I returned from work and noticed that Heidi's dog house was slanting over on its side. Upon closer examination, I discovered that Heidi had taken it upon herself to go into the construction business and add a basement to her dog house. There was a gigantic hole, approximately six feet by three feet, under one side of the dog house, causing the dog house to lean precariously from the top rim of the hole. I quickly filled in the hole, but it was almost a daily ritual for me to fill in big holes in the back yard.

One day, the landlord stopped by, and for some reason, he drove around the house and into the back yard. I had not quite filled in all the holes that day. Jan and I both cringed. The landlord's big station wagon looked rather comical, moving across the back yard, bumping up and down as he traversed the holes. I thought that he might get stuck, because of some of the larger holes, but he did not, and he didn't say a word. He was a very considerate guy. I think he appreciated having tenants who paid their rent on time and took good care of his property (except for those back yard craters, of course).

Heidi once gave us another moment of watchdog humor, when we drove from Charleston to Iowa to visit Jan's parents. Heidi came with us and slept on the floor in our bedroom. Sometime during the night, Jan's dad walked past our bedroom door, and Heidi didn't rise, but she emitted a loud and scary, deep German Shepherd growl. We did not hear it, because we were sleeping so soundly. The next morning, Jan's dad grumbled around at breakfast and finally blurted out, "Damn it, a man can't even walk around in his own house at night without getting snarled at!" It was all Jan and I could do to suppress our laughter. We knew Heidi was just a big sissy in a German Shepherd fur coat.

Part Two

Iron Men and Wooden Ships

The USS Rival (MSO-468)

Any ship can be a minesweeper—once!

—Author unknown

MINESWEEPERS are part of what I call the unglorious, "working Navy." By my own definition, working Navy ships are primarily non-combatant ships. As such, they do not garner glory. They are the working Navy because what they do is dirty, tough, and extremely dangerous work, serving the sometimes elitist, front-line combatant Navy units.

In the case of minesweepers, the favorite slogan of minesweeper sailors is, "Iron Men in Wooden Ships." And that slogan is really true. Guys (and now women) in the working Navy will always have the tongue-in-cheek attitude that they work a lot harder on working type ships than personnel on other types of ships. Even as part of the working Navy, minesweepers are somewhat nearer the point of the spear, because without their efforts, other ships cannot safely enter an area that is known to have been mined. Minesweepers play a necessary and dangerous role in keeping the sea lanes open. Yet, they have armament only for their own protection or for detonating mines, so they are not considered combatants. For the Navy's purposes, minesweepers are classified in their own category—minesweeping craft. But sweep sailors please forgive me. For my purposes I am going to discuss my minesweeping adventures right along with my auxiliary ship stories.

The Vietnam era ocean going minesweepers (MSOs) were mission oriented, unique Navy ships. First and foremost, they were made of wood. Unlike the thick steel hulls of other Navy ships, thick oak planking made up the outer hull of the MSO. All of the major framework of the ship, including the keel and all ribs of the ship were also made of wood. As much as was possible, all of the metal fittings, deck gear, and minesweeping gear, were either made of brass or stainless steel. Electrical machinery on the ship was housed in special shielding. The reason for all this was that a minesweeper needed to be as non-ferrous as possible; that is, non-magnetic. Many of the mines designed to destroy passing ships have a magnetically activated trigger mechanism. A disturbance of the ocean's magnetic field by a steel ship passing by could set off a magnetic mine. The theory was that a wooden ship would not disturb that magnetic field, and the MSO could pass by safely, neutralizing the magnetic mine by use of mine counter measures.

Additionally, the old MSO minesweeper carried an assortment of mine countermeasure equipment, which was heavy, cumbersome, and had to be manually rigged, streamed out, and towed behind the ship as it carried out its duties of finding and disabling mines. It is heavy, dirty, extremely tiring, and above all, dangerous work. The purpose of this equipment is to counter the threat of different types of mines. For instance, there are magnetic mines, which I just described. To counteract the magnetic mine, a minesweeper would tow a special array that changes the earth's magnetic field in the immediate area as it passes through the water. When the magnetic mine detected this magnetic change, it detonated, but the non-ferrous minesweeper towing the array was safely out of range as it had already passed by the mine. However, in order for that procedure to be successful, the MSO must have emitted only a negligible magnetic signature of its own. For that reason, the MSOs were tested in a special degaussing process to measure the amount of magnetic field being generated by the ship. About twice a year, each MSO would be piloted through a special degaussing range. As the ship moved through the range, underwater instruments and cables would measure the amount of magnetism emitted by the ship. If the measurement was within safe levels, the MSO would be declared safe for operation against magnetic mines.

Then there are acoustic mines. These mines lay in wait for a passing ship, listening for the characteristic sounds of a ship's engines and turning screw in the water. When the mine hears these noises at a preprogrammed signature and decibel level signifying that the target ship is within range, it detonates and damages or sinks the passing ship. To counter this threat, a minesweeper towed a large, heavy device that made acoustically pulsing sounds similar to the sounds of a large ship going through the water. Again, if the sounds made by this device being towed were similar to and loud enough for the mine's pre-set program, the mine would harmlessly detonate after the passing minesweeper was clear.

A third type of mine is the contact mine. These are the mines always depicted in the Hollywood Navy movies. You will remember, these are the mines tethered by cable or chain to float just under the surface. The mines usually have "horns" on them that an unsuspecting ship or submarine bumps into, thereby detonating the mine. The minesweeper towed a special type of cable cutter attached to the towed array. As this cutter caught the cable or chain of the suspended mine, the cutter severed the cable and the mine floated to the surface where the minesweeper could use its armament to shoot the mine and detonate it.

One other mine was the counting mine. This mine might be any combination of the aforementioned mines, but it also has a counting device built into the mine. Hence, it has the ability to count the number of ships that have passed by the mine, and would only detonate when its pre-programmed number is reached. For example, if the internal counter in the mine was set at five, the mine would only detonate as the fifth ship passed by.

In 1969 when I joined the USS Rival, these mine types and their associated Navy mine countermeasure procedures and theories were still in use, and they were the primary methods used to successfully clear mines from a mine field at sea. Today, mines are much more sophisticated, but there are also better means by which to disable them, including mine countermeasure ships and helicopter minesweeping, both of which undoubtedly have much more sophisticated search and destroy capabilities and are immensely safer for their operators.

For perspective and information purposes, below are some specifications about the USS Rival (MSO-468):

USS Rival (MSO-468) with her crew "Manning the Rail"[9]

The Rival's career[10]

Laid down	February 1, 1952
Launched	August 15, 1953
Commissioned	September 3, 1954

---

[9] NAVSOURCE Naval History, Photographic History of the U.S. Navy, http://www. NAVSOURCE.org/archives/11/02468.htm.

[10] Ibid.

Decommissioned	May 15, 1970
Struck from the Navy roles	February 1, 1971
Homeport	Charleston, SC
Fate	Sold for scrap August 1971

The Rival's characteristics[11]

Displacement	775 tons
Length	172 feet
Beam	36 feet
Draught	10 feet
Top Speed	15 knots
Complement	6 Officers 70 Enlisted
Armament	One 40mm mount and small arms
Propulsion	4 Waukasha Motors Diesels, Twin Screw, Variable pitch propellers

In May 1969, I reported aboard the USS Rival (MSO-468) for my first military active duty in the Vietnam era. With a knot in my stomach, I climbed up the gangway and saluted the ensign (the U.S. flag flying at the stern of the ship), a custom followed by all Navy personnel coming on board a Navy ship. Next, I saluted the quarterdeck watch, which is also a custom when coming on board a Navy ship, and asked for permission to come aboard. I then stepped aboard my first Navy ship in which I was to serve.

As a volunteer junior Naval officer during the Vietnam war, the Navy in all its wisdom had sent me to a non-combatant ship on the east coast of the United States, half the globe away from the on-going war in Vietnam. There would be no battle conditions for me during an unglorious tour in Charleston, South Carolina. I was a bit disappointed, but I also knew that if I were to make the Navy a career, a small ship, where each officer served as a department head, was excellent training, and I looked forward to the hard work.

I was directed to the ship's office, which is where you can normally find a ship's Executive Officer (XO), the second in command of a Navy ship. The XO functions as the CO of the ship in the absence of the Captain (the commanding officer of a Navy ship is called the Captain of the ship, no matter what his/her rank is). The XO is also the administrative

---

[11] Ibid.

officer of the ship. It is pretty well known in the Navy that if there is to be a "good cop, bad cop" scenario on the ship, the XO is almost always the Captain's enforcer. So sometimes, for subordinates, the XO is a bit harder to live with onboard than the CO.

Lieutenant Beau

I knocked on the ship's office door, and someone growled and told me to enter. I now met Lieutenant (LT) Beau. LT Beau was a Southern gentleman from Louisiana. He chain smoked and seldom smiled when talking to the junior officers. He usually just growled out orders or remedial "guidance." He scared the hell out of this brand new ensign. It seemed like he was always mad at me, and I could do nothing correct in his eyes. The other junior officers also had a healthy respect for the XO.

The Rival had six officers and around seventy enlisted men on board. In addition to the CO and XO, the junior officers were Ensign Ben, Lieutenant Junior Grade (LTJG) Ken, and LTJG Rick. LTJG Rick was the senior of our little group of four junior officers, and he had been on board the Rival the longest. Hence, he was the "go to" guy for me for all my questions; and I had a million of them. Rick was the Deck/Minesweeping Officer. The leading Deck Officer on a ship is also called "The First Lieutenant."[12] (If I do not have you confused by now, you just aren't paying attention!) So Rick's position was usually just referred to as the First Lieutenant. LTJG Ken was the Operations Officer, in charge of communications and exercise (ship's movement) planning. Ensign Ben was the Engineering Officer, in charge of all the machinery and propulsion gear of the ship. It was his responsibility to make sure the ship was in good running order. The head Engineering Officer on a Navy ship is called "Cheng," a derivative of the Chief Engineer title, and is sometimes pronounced Chang. LTJG Rick is another of my unsung heroes. Because of his patience and expertise, I was able to learn quickly, the knowledge and tasks I would need to be successful in my role on the Rival.

Captain Bob

The final player in the wardroom gang was the CO, Lieutenant Commander Bob. Remember, no matter what the rank, the Commanding Officer of a Navy ship is called Captain by all individuals on that ship. If I quaked near the XO, the CO really scared me. Captain Bob also chain smoked and spoke very loudly. If he laughed, you could hear him from far away. He seldom addressed you to your face. He always seemed to be

---

[12] First Lieutenant, Wikipedia, http://en.wikipedia.org/wik/First_Lieutenant.

talking to the XO when he was talking about one of the junior officers. Pretty easy to see why Navy junior officers all have inferiority complexes. But Captain Bob was very typical of career Navy officers at that time. He was a Lieutenant Commander, and to have reached that rank, he would have had from eight to ten years in the Navy. So, he was a career officer; or as the enlisted sailors used to say, "He's a lifer!"

It was important that a career officer avoid circumstances that would jeopardize his career. The career officer's annual fitness report, written by his senior, could make or break a career and keep an officer from being promoted. All of this had to weigh heavily on the career officer, and this stress contributed greatly to the huge number of Navy officers who smoked and drank alcohol, sometimes to excess. It was just the way it was. I had quit smoking prior to entering OCS in order to be in good physical condition, but onboard the ship, nearly everyone smoked, and I took up the habit again and was soon back to being a two-pack-a-day guy.

Captain Bob was a hard charger and had aspirations of later promotion. His previous jobs in the Navy had involved serving on a destroyer. That experience is always a good path to later securing a CO job, like that on the Rival. He was also very "hands on" when dealing with even the minutiae of the day-to-day operations of the ship. When the Rival was underway, it was apparent he loved every minute of it, but still, he did not relax and continued to pace the deck, barking orders. It was best to stay away from him if you were not needed at the moment.

I was assigned to be the Supply Officer on the Rival when I reported on board. The Navy has a separate classification of officers who go through a special Supply Corps School, and they are then assigned to the Navy Supply Corps and serve duty on larger Navy ships or at shore supply depots. I was not a supply officer; I was a Line Officer. Only a Line Officer can hold command of a Navy ship at sea. But on small ships, which do not have a Supply Corps Officer, a Line Officer may be designated as the ship's supply officer in order to ensure accountability for the ship's purchases and acquisitions.

In the officer hierarchy of the ship, the supply officer carries the least clout and panache. That job was almost always given to the newest and most junior officer when he came aboard. To assume the Rival's Supply Officer job, I needed to attend a special school held on the Charleston base for small afloat commands to learn at least the basics of supply management afloat. So, very soon after reporting to the Rival in 1969, I was assigned to take the supply course. The course lasted approximately three weeks.

A Supply Officer on a ship holds the purse strings of the ship. As the Supply Department Head, I had charge of all purchasing of everything needed on the ship from parts to food items. In addition, I had charge of the galley (kitchen), the mess decks (dining areas) the mess men (cooks and cooks' helpers), the storekeepers (supply clerks who ordered all material used on the ship), and the stewards (the staff who took care of the officers' wardroom and cleaned the wardroom and officers' quarters).

Our two stewards were Filipino men, and they were always fun to talk with about their country. But stewards were not very well respected by the rest of the crew, because they waited on the officers of the ship. They were sometimes disrespectfully called "Officer Table Navigators," or sometimes worse. But they did their best to make life a bit easier in the wardroom, and we liked them.

It was also mandatory that every new officer coming on board the minesweepers complete a minesweeping course. I began this course immediately following the supply course. The course was roughly four weeks long and taught the new officers the rudiments of all the gear on an MSO, and how all the equipment was to be used to hunt and disarm mines. It was a good course, and I enjoyed it.

Bear in mind that any military service during the Vietnam era was not always respected, even by some of the men serving at the time. We had often heard the front line troops were not happy to be in Vietnam, as evidenced by some of the illegal drug use, disrespect for authority, and other actions. But having recently graduated from Navy Officer Candidate School, where we were all volunteers, I had not seen any of this dissatisfaction first hand, until attending the aforementioned minesweeping school. As it happened, in class I sat next to a LTJG named Jerry, who had just come from another type of ship and was being transferred to an MSO. Jerry and I hit it off, but I soon learned that he was not happy that the military was interrupting his life (he was a law school graduate), even though he had volunteered to be in the Navy. He was convinced that most of what we learned or did in the Navy was a lot of male bovine excrement. Although I also thought there were some rather inane Navy practices and procedures, I was different from Jerry in the fact that I liked the Navy and wanted to make it a career. So we had some rather strange conversations, wherein he derided the service, and I feebly gave the Navy faint praise in order to avoid arguments. In retrospect, it seems odd that we became good friends, and our wives became good friends too. They were a fun couple, and we got together with them socially on many occasions. This was one of the first individuals I had met in the Navy who was not necessarily happy to be serving his country. I met many others in the military who were not happy to be in uniform, but I was never swayed from my own opinions.

Ensign Indoctrination

Two ensigns are standing on the deck of the sinking ship. The ship was rapidly going down. One ensign turns to the other and says, "What are we going to do?" The other ensign says, "Let's swim for it." The first ensign says, "But I can't swim!" His buddy then says, "We're ensigns. We'll do what we always do—FAKE IT!"

—Author unknown

Depending upon the individual ship's practice, it is common that each new ensign who comes aboard his first ship is hazed and teased by the other officers, and sometimes tactfully by the enlisted guys. That's just the way it is. But I was not aware of that until it was my turn. Being the new guy on the Rival, I was always being quizzed by the XO or the CO as they attempted to trip me up or just prove how stupid new ensigns really are. Some of it was fun, and I laughed along with them when I would say something stupidly wrong.

But some of the razzing was a bit frustrating. We were at sea off the coast of Charleston for local operations (local ops). As we cruised off the coast, I was standing watch under instruction to learn how to operate the ship. All of this bridge training is to afford the junior officer the opportunity to learn how to be a qualified officer of the deck (OOD). I'll explain that later. Anyway, the CO was in his chair (every Navy ship has a big comfortable swivel pedestal chair on the bridge for the Captain.) The Rival had a CO's chair and a much smaller chair for the XO. The CO and XO were conferring, and I was only paying attention to LTJG Rick, from whom I was receiving instruction.

Suddenly I heard from the Captain, "Mr. Duermeyer!"

Another, oh, crap moment. "Yes, Sir," I replied.

The Captain then said, "Mr. Duermeyer, as Supply Officer, your office holds the key to the motor whaleboat."

The motor whaleboat was a motorized life boat, which hung on davits that could be swung out to drop the boat on cables to the surface of the sea for use by ship personnel.

The Captain continued, "This afternoon, we are going to have an exercise to launch the motor whaleboat and pick up a simulated man overboard. We will need the key to the motor whaleboat. Go get it and bring it to me."

"Yes, sir," I responded, and took off for my stateroom. I shared a stateroom with Ensign Ben. Our stateroom was about the size of a medium sized closet—two bunks and a bit of cupboard space. So there was not that much area to search. I looked and looked for any key that might have promise. I found nothing. I then went to see my storekeeper clerk, because he pretty much knew everything about the Supply Department. He denied holding the whaleboat key and said that he thought I had it. Dead end. He then suggested that since it was a key to a boat with a motor, that I should check with some of the enginemen in the engine room. So I then climbed down the ladder (the navy calls stairs, ladders) into the bowels of the ship into the dirty, smelly, noisy engine room. Man, you could not hear anything down there it was so loud with those four huge Waukasha diesel main engines and the generators running. I finally spotted Ensign Ben and leaned into him to yell in his ear. I told him that the CO had requested that I bring the key to the motor whaleboat to him and asked Ben if he had it, or if he knew where it was. He said he did not have it and did not know its whereabouts. He suggested that I go up to chiefs' quarters and knock on their door and ask them.

I was not enthused by his suggestion, because I figured the chiefs would not necessarily feel an obligation to help this poor green ensign. But I headed for the "Goat Locker" (Navy jargon for chiefs' quarters.) I climbed back onto the main deck and went around to the starboard side to rap on the door to the Goat Locker.

The Rival had two chiefs onboard. They were an engineman (EN) chief, and an electrician's mate (EM) chief. And the Rival, being so small, also had the first class petty officers bunk in with the chiefs. The Engineman Chief was in their quarters, and I asked him about the whaleboat key. He said he did not have it and suggested that I ask First Class Boatswain's Mate, Ernie. So I found Boats (the leading boatswain's mates on ships are usually just called "Boats") on the fantail of the ship and talked with him. Ernie grinned suspiciously and said he had no idea where the key was.

Now this was a little strange, because the boatswain's mates are the persons who actually drive the whaleboat when it is in the water. Oh man, if they did not know where the key was, it was really lost.

Now, I was frantic. The CO was waiting for me on the bridge to bring him that key. I was so desperate that I started asking everyone that I passed on the ship if they knew where the key was. Everyone pleaded ignorance. In a bit, one of the third class enginemen came up from the engine room for some fresh air as I was standing by the engine room ladder. He stood there a moment, lit up a smoke, and looked at me. He saw how I was in a real state of frustration and worry. He nodded his head and made a motion for me to follow him. We stood on the fantail and he explained to me.

"Mr. Duermeyer," he said, "there is no such thing as a key to the motor whaleboat. It is started by just pushing a button."

I had been had by my CO and the other members of the wardroom. Boatswain's Mate Ernie was standing to the side watching us, and he saw my reaction and burst out laughing. Not only did the officers know how stupid I was, but most of the crew also knew.

But then Ernie came over to me, and he put his big old crusty boatswain's mate paw on my shoulder and said, "Now Mr. Duermeyer, don't take it so hard. You'll learn the ropes, and we will make a Fleet Ensign (an ensign who knows what the heck is going on onboard a ship) out of you yet." And he just smiled and took a drag on his Pall Mall.

Well, he made me feel a bit better, but I still had to climb up on the bridge and face the CO, and by this time I was mad. I climbed up to the bridge and walked over to the CO's chair.

He swiveled around and said, "Well, Mr. Duermeyer. Where's the key?" Everyone on the bridge was watching me and my reaction.

I said, "Captain, it is my understanding that there is no key to the motor whaleboat. The boat can be started with a starter button."

Everyone on the bridge had a good laugh at the new ensign's ignorance. Boy, was I mad!

There were other such occasions for jokes at my expense, but they did not go on forever. I remember the final such occasion when I was on the bridge with the CO and XO, and the Captain again barked, "Mr. Duermeyer!" Oh, crap, not again...

I answered, "Yes, sir."

The Captain then said, "Jim, we need to better secure this awning over the bridge. It is loose in one corner."

Again I said, "Yes, sir."

He went on, "Go down to your Supply Office and get the Storekeeper to give you six fathoms of that special waterproof water line." (Remember in Navy lingo, rope is line.)

I responded, "Yes, sir, I'll go get it for you."

I climbed down the ladder and headed for the Supply Office. But before I got to the Supply Office, it hit me. Water line is the line painted all along the side of a ship to mark the normal height of the surface of the water on the ship. Once again, I'd been had. But I had an idea.

I went directly to the fantail and found Boats. He was working his best marlinspike seamanship on some heavy line, weaving large loops in the end of the line so that it could be used as a mooring line.

I asked him, "Boats, can you give me about ten feet of light nylon line, preferably white in color?"

Boats said, "Sure, what do you want it for?"

I would not tell him, but he cut off the line I wanted from a spool in the boatswain's locker. Now, I had piqued the curiosity of one of the leading enlisted men on the ship. As I slowly climbed back up to the bridge, I kept the line hidden behind my back. I walked over to the Captain's chair.

The Captain barked, "Well, did you get my water line?"

I quickly brought the length of line from around my back and handed it to the CO.

In dead seriousness, I then said, "Yes sir, this is the finest waterproof water line that we had in the boatswains' locker. I hope it will meet your needs."

The Captain looked at me, looked at the line I had given him (literally and figuratively), and looked back at me without a smile. He knew his joke had not quite worked this time. Before he could say anything I quickly walked off the bridge and down the ladder. I stopped just out of sight at the base of the ladder, and in a minute, I heard the Captain and XO loudly laughing. I got away with it! Word of my little joke spread throughout the ship, and that was the end of the pranks pulled on the green ensign.

When I saw Boats later that day, he said, "Can I have my water line back?"

We both had a good laugh.

The Bull Ensign

On every Navy ship, the most senior of the ensigns is given the honorary title of "Bull Ensign." It is a silly old tradition, that I believe is perpetuated by the ship's senior officers as just another way to poke fun of the dumb ensigns. A couple of months after I came aboard the Rival, Ensign Ben was promoted to LTJG. That left me as the only ensign on board. Navy ensigns are the equivalent of other military branch's second lieutenant. As such, an ensign wears a small gold bar on each collar point of the uniform shirt.

One day, the XO caught me in the wardroom at lunch, and in front of the other officers, he presented me with the biggest set of gold bars for my collar that I had ever seen. They were at least three times longer and wider than the normal gold collar pin. Not only that, but the word "BULL" was engraved on them. The XO then told me that as the official Bull Ensign, I would need to wear them at all times. Everyone had another good laugh at the expense of the ensign. How embarrassing! So,

I went about my duties on the ship wearing these ridiculous collar bars for probably a week. After that, I quietly replaced those bars with my real gold uniform bars, and the XO did not seem to care. He had had his fun.

OODs

An ensign was sitting for his first qualification board for Officer of the Deck at sea. He had already answered a large number of difficult questions, but the Captain decided to put the ensign in a completely hypothetical emergency situation. "What would you do if the ship lost power and a sudden storm sprang up on the starboard side," the Captain asked. "Throw out an anchor, Sir," the ensign replied. "And what would you do if another storm sprang up aft?" "I'd throw out another anchor, Captain." The Captain then asked, "If a third terrific storm sprang up, what would you do then?" The ensign said, "Throw out another anchor." "Hold on," said the Captain. "Where are you getting all these anchors from?" The ensign smiled and said, "From the same place you're getting all those storms, Sir."

—Author unknown

The Navy Officers who are responsible for driving a ship and giving orders to maneuver a ship are called Line Officers. Line Officers are the only officers who are eligible to have command of a ship. Line Officer uniforms have a star on their sleeve or shoulder board to designate the wearer as a Line Officer. The term Line Officer dates back to the eighteenth century when sailing ships formed lines to attack each other using their broadside guns. Navy Line Officers sometimes refer to themselves in slang, as "ship drivers." All the officers on the Rival were Line Officers.

The Captain of a Navy ship is ultimately responsible for his ship. That means that ANYTHING that happens to that ship is the responsibility of the Captain. But the Captain cannot be in all places at all times on a ship. Therefore, at times, the Captain delegates some of the authority for the ship to another officer on the ship. When that responsibility is for driving the ship or acting in the absence of the Captain, the responsibility generally falls to the XO or to the Officer of the Deck (OOD). If the Captain has not formally given this authority to another officer, it is always assumed that the Captain is the OOD.

During my active duty days in the Navy, there were three Officer of the Deck (OOD) qualifications. First, was OOD in port (OODI); next was OOD underway (OODU); and finally there was OOD fleet (OODF). If an officer was classified in one of these ratings, it meant that the officer had that rating only on the ship on which he/she qualified. For example, being a qualified OOD on a minesweeper did not transfer if the officer transferred to an aircraft carrier. He/she would have to requalify on the new ship.

It was the goal of every Navy officer to receive the OODF designation for the ship in which they were serving. That rating meant that you were qualified to command your ship while underway in formation with, or operating with, other ships.

Every Navy ship has a group of persons on duty at all times. This group of people makes up the duty section. While the ship is in port, the duty section is comprised of the personnel who remain on the ship overnight to maintain the security and safety of the ship. At sea, it is usually the duty section which is actually carrying out the specific jobs to facilitate operating the ship, while the remainder of personnel are either resting or on other projects on the ship. The terminology for being a part of the duty section is that you "have the duty," or you are "standing duty," or, you've "got the dudes." Also, on every Navy ship in port, the duty section almost always includes a Line Officer in the section, so that there is an officer responsible for the safety and security of the ship at all times. On the Rival and the other MSOs in Charleston, the four junior officers rotated the in port overnight duty. The CO and XO did not stand overnight duty in port.

As soon as I came aboard, my training for OODI began. The other three junior officers wanted me trained as quickly as possible, so that they could stand duty one night in four, instead of one in three. So I stood duty with LTJG Rick on the nights he had duty so that he could teach me all that I would need to know to be responsible for the ship in port.

At that time, the qualification procedure was different than it is today. When the training officer felt that the new officer was ready, the new officer reported to the XO, and the XO would fire a series of questions at the officer to see if the new officer was ready to stand duty by himself. Usually, the XO would flunk the new officer the first time and make him stand a few more nights under instruction.

The XO would bellow, "You think you are ready for me to turn responsibility for this $65 million ship to you. Wrong, you're not ready, and you may never be ready."

The other junior officers knew the game, and they also knew that very shortly I would be qualified. Soon there were four of us who were qualified, so we stood one-in-four duty. The next hurdle would be to undergo training to become qualified at sea.

When a Navy ship is getting underway or is at sea, it is not always the Captain who is driving the ship. He can delegate the responsibility for driving the ship to a qualified OODU, so that he does not have to be on the bridge at all times. To further complicate this picture, the OODU can further delegate some of this responsibility. He can delegate responsibility to another qualified officer to give all orders for driving the ship, while the OOD oversees. He, thus, has given the responsibility to a "Conning Officer or control officer." At this point I know I have you thoroughly confused. That's all right, you are learning some of the things that a new ensign had to learn when he came on board. When there is an OOD and a Conning Officer on the bridge, the enlisted personnel who carry out the orders have to know who is giving the driving orders. As each officer assumes his respective responsibility, he shouts out his name to the enlisted staff on the bridge, saying, "I have the Deck," or "I have the Conn."

There is a ritual that OODs must go through at the end of each watch on the bridge. The officer who is to relieve the OOD goes to the bridge and reads any message traffic that has come in pertaining to the ship. He then looks at the navigation chart to see exactly where the ship is and the nature of the water in which the ship will travel. Will the ship travel in shallow water, deep water, any reefs, etc.? After all of these facts have been passed to the relieving OOD, the officer is ready to take over the OOD watch.

He announces to the acting OOD, "I am ready to relieve you sir."

The active OOD announces, "I am ready to be relieved."

At this point the active OOD briefs the oncoming officer and tells him which engines are running, which ship generators and other equipment are operating, the course and speed of the ship, special orders from the CO or XO, and all other items that the OOD needs to know to assume operation of the ship.

When the relieving OOD is comfortable that he knows all of the pertinent data, he announces, "I relieve you, sir," and the active OOD replies, "I stand relieved." The new OOD then announces to everyone on the bridge, "This is (Rank and Name), and I have the deck," which means that he is now the active OOD on duty.

With this ritual, every watch stander on the bridge and everyone throughout the ship knows the identity of the OOD who is on the bridge and in charge of the operation of the ship. These procedures represent the practice followed by the ships on which I served. OOD relieving procedures on other ships may have varied somewhat from what I have described.

One last item, I sometimes tend to simplify and call the operation of the ship, driving the ship. Actual orders given by the OOD or Conning Officer to operate the ship are called orders to the helm. The helm refers to the ship's wheel, compass, and engine order telegraph, and the personnel manning these stations. The ship's helm is usually close by on the bridge for the OOD to give the helm orders.

Sea Detail

Before coming aboard the Rival, I had never been on an ocean-going ship, so the prospect of heading out to sea was exciting to me. I wondered about getting seasick and asked LTJG Rick about it. He said to get some little pink Dramamine pills from the corpsman and take one of those about thirty minutes before the ship was to get underway. I followed his advice.

At the appointed time, an announcement was made throughout the ship. "All hands report to sea detail!" Men started scrambling throughout the ship and went to their designated place on the ship to perform their specific job to get the ship underway.

As the lowly new ensign, I stood at the back of the bridge to observe all of the activity, so that I could learn how to qualify as an OOD and have the responsibility for getting the ship underway. Initially, it was daunting to watch all of the orchestrated moves involved in getting a ship underway. I could hear all of the orders given to the helm that would be transferred to the engine room, to the command information center, and to the deck personnel. In addition to the helm personnel, there are always headset telephone talkers relaying all orders to the various locations on the ship where the orders will be carried out. This redundancy ensures that the OOD's orders are understood by everyone. Each man had a job to do, but it had to be done in a correct sequence by following the orders of the Officer of the Deck who had control of the ship. It appeared to be a sort of bumbling, military, sailor-guy choreography. No fancy dance steps, but the play was carried out. The proper engines and generators were running, the communications were checked out, all hands were in their proper places doing their jobs, and finally the commands were given to cast off part of the lines holding the ship to the pier. Then commands were given to twist the ship away from the pier by running one screw forward and one backward while still tied to the pier with one line (called a spring line). The ship slowly moved its stern away from the pier, and then the ship was backed slowly away from the pier into the open river while the final line was taken aboard.

Charleston, South Carolina, lies at the confluence of two rivers, the Ashley and the Cooper. At that time, the Naval base was located five miles up the twisting and turning Cooper river on the west bank of the river. To move any ship from the Navy base to open sea took considerable maneuvering down this serpentine river to finally reach the sea.

All the while the ship was moving toward the sea, the ship remained at sea detail. The reason for this was that if anything unexpected occurred, the heightened number of crewmen on sea detail could attend to the emergency in the restricted waters leading to the ocean. Sea Detail on the Rival, leaving or entering Charleston Harbor would usually last at least a full hour.

Getting a ship from the Naval Base to the sea was a good test of an OOD's conning abilities. The river was treacherous. There were always wicked tidal currents and swift flow in the river. The course on the river was full of turns for the ship, and the river was narrow in places. All of these things kept the conning officer busy adjusting the course and speed of the ship as it moved down river. In addition, there were always cargo and petroleum ships plying the river on their way north to Charleston warehouses and terminals to off-load their cargo. As I watched the CO and the OOD maneuver the Rival to the open ocean, I found it fascinating, and I recognized the skill involved in driving a ship. Plus, it looked like a great deal of fun! I wanted to learn this as quickly as I could.

LTJG Rick took me under his wing once again and had me stand beside him as we took the ship to sea on numerous occasions, and within a couple of months, I was ready to take the ship to sea by myself. After this skill was accomplished and I could show the Captain that I was capable, I would be further quizzed before being given the OODU qualification. Even after I had passed the test and qualified, Captain Bob always seemed nervous whenever he allowed one of the junior officers to land the ship at the base piers (maybe more so when I was driving).

Landing a ship at a pier is always a nerve wracking experience. One mistake can wreck the ship and tear apart a pier, not to mention destroy a career. Charleston was always a difficult landing because of the tidal current and river flow, coupled with any wind. Captain Bob would pace the bridge whenever a subordinate was conning, and you could see him biting his tongue to keep from jumping in and taking over. He would be constantly giving advice to the conning officer, which made this conning officer very nervous. I operate better when people are not telling me how to do something. I prefer that my instructor watch me and advise me *when necessary*. Anyway, over time, I acquired the necessary skills and gained the OODU qualification.

My concern about whether I would suffer seasickness was answered fairly quickly on the first time we went to sea. Oh yeah, I got sick. But like everyone else, I soon gained my sea legs and became accustomed to the ride of the minesweeper. But this would not be the last time I was seasick. More on that later.

When the Rival went to sea, we occasionally operated alone, but often we were with another minesweeper or two. If we were with other sweeps, it was common for our squadron commodore, a commander in rank, to accompany us for a day or more. He often rode the Rival, and he would take charge of running an exercise for participation by all of the sweeps. This usually involved the sweeps being in formation and carrying out simulated minesweeping by using specialized towing gear for different types of mines. It was impressive to see the minesweepers operating in formation, while towing their gear over a simulated mine field.

During minesweeping exercises, the hub of activity shifted from the bridge to the stern or fantail of the ship. All the rigging of the minesweeping equipment was done on the fantail, and then streamed from the stern of the ship. The mine countermeasure equipment was lashed down on various cradles on the fantail. Each piece of gear had to be lifted by crane, attached in its proper location on the streaming wires, and then lowered into the water as the ship progressed through the water. Sounds easy, doesn't it? Now, consider that the ship's fantail is moving up and down over the waves and is rocking side to side. So the heavy equipment, while suspended, is swinging back and forth over a constantly moving platform. Some of this gear weighed as much as a thousand pounds. Imagine an old time Volkswagen car swinging on a cable above your head, while you work underneath it on a floor that never is stationary. You get the picture. The boatswain's mates had to attach other equipment to the piece that was swinging around by using shackles, which had to be attached and tightened before other equipment was added. Finally, the entire apparatus would be lowered off the stern of the ship and streamed aft of the ship. With wire cable and rope strung all over the fantail, suspended heavy equipment, and a heaving ocean, rigging the minesweeping equipment was extremely dangerous work. A slip or break in a cable could crush a man or cause serious injury. It was the First Lieutenant's job to oversee this activity and ensure that every action took place in a safe environment. All fantail personnel wore hard hats, life vests, safety glasses, leather gloves, and all loose clothing was tucked in or taped off. But even taking all possible safety measures, it was fairly common for one of the deck gang to get a cut, a gash, or to smash a hand or finger. No serious injuries occurred during my time on the minesweepers, but all personnel working around the fantail and the sweep gear had to be extremely cautious. These were unsung heroes placing themselves in harm's way, carrying out their assigned duties.

Prior to my arrival, the Rival had a long and busy history. The ship had visited many countries in Northern European waters and the Mediterranean Sea, participating in many exercises with the U.S. Navy and other NATO countries. The ship took a "Med cruise" about every eighteen months, and I was looking forward to seeing some foreign countries in the next year or so. I did not know it yet, but this would not happen.

We continued our local operations off Charleston, and I continued my training for OODF. During one period while we were at sea, the exercise we were conducting lasted for several days. Each night, we anchored at sea. While the ship was not underway at sea, we had an "anchor watch" duty section. This meant there were not as many people on bridge watch, because the ship was not underway. In this situation, the main responsibility of the OOD and the bridge watch team was to take bearings from the ship to ensure that the ship's anchor was holding and to keep a sharp lookout for merchant ships traversing near us in the night. We could check our position by taking bearings on two navigational lights that were visible off the coast of Charleston. If the bearings remained the same at each sighting, then we knew the ship's anchor was holding the ship in position. If we sighted merchant ships or other ships which might approach our anchored position too closely, we were to notify the CO at once.

One of those evenings while we were at anchor off the coast, I had the OOD mid-watch. The mid-watch is the midnight to four a.m. watch (0000-0400). I was on the bridge with a quartermaster of the watch, a boatswain's mate of the watch, and a phone talker/runner, primarily taking bearings every fifteen minutes. It had been a tough day, and I was really tired. The time on watch dragged on. At about 0200, the fatigue finally got to me, and I decided that I could maintain the watch and sit in the XO's chair. These were two really big no-nos! You were *never to* sit down on watch, and junior officers were *not allowed* to sit in the CO or XO's chair. I was sitting in the chair being rocked gently back and forth by the ship's motion. As a result, I became sleepier as time went by.

The ladder up to the bridge was behind the XO's chair, so it was not visible to me. Suddenly I heard a bellowing voice say, "Mr. Duermeyer!"

Oh crap! I flew out of the chair and landed on my rear on the deck. It was the XO. What was he doing up on the bridge at this hour?

"What the hell do you think you're doing, sitting down on watch and sitting in my chair," bellowed LT Beau.

I was really in it this time. The bellowing and chewing and spitting went on for an eternity. I had been chewed down to about one foot tall by the end of the XO's tirade. Another lesson learned the hard way. You can bet I never did that again.

Driving an MSO

Driving an MSO is unlike driving other Navy ships. All of us are familiar from movies when the hero shouts out things like, "All ahead full," or "all ahead standard," or "all back full." Those commands mean full speed or standard speed. On an MSO, the commands to the helm might sound like this, "all ahead one foot," or "all ahead two feet," or "all back two feet." On any other ship, the speed of the ship is changed by changing the speed of the propeller (in the Navy, a propeller is also called a screw). The faster the revolution of the propeller, the faster the ship goes. But on an MSO, the propellers rotate at a constant rate. The speed of the propeller does not change. What does change is the pitch of the blades of the propeller. The propeller blades actually pivot to increase or decrease the pitch of the propeller. When the pitch increases, the propeller pulls more water through and past the propeller. So if the helm order is, "all ahead one foot," that means that the pitch of both propellers should be set to bring one foot of water through the propellers with each revolution of the propellers. By increasing the pitch of the propeller, more water can be brought through the turning propeller, thereby increasing the speed of the ship. Now, how is all of that for developing a party trivia question? In addition, like most larger Navy ships, the MSOs had twin screws, thereby enabling the ship to be very maneuverable, a property that was invaluable when sweeping for dangerous mines.

During an underway watch, the OOD who drove the ship would be located on the bridge, which was an awning covered deck above the pilot house deck. The helm was in the pilot house, alongside the engine order telegraph. The OOD would shout his conning orders down a speaker tube that terminated just above the head of the helmsman (the man turning the ship's steering wheel). In addition, a phone talker relayed the same orders by telephone to a talker in the pilot house. The personnel on the helm would repeat the orders back to the OOD, signifying that the order was heard and was being carried out. Duplicity ensured that the orders given by the OOD were understood and carried out correctly.

The OOD had a little platform on which he stood so that he could see out all the windows on the bridge. His speaking tube was built into one side of the platform. But if the OOD wanted to move out to a wing of the bridge where he could look back onto the fantail or down the side of the ship or to the front of the ship, he simply took his phone talker out on the wing with him, and the orders were relayed by phone.

Gunnery Practice

If the enemy is in range, so are you!

—Author unknown

In theory, an MSO had the ability to shoot any floating mines and blow them up so that they would not be a hazard to other ships. The MSO should also have the ability to fire at any airplane attacking the ship. However, the armament carried on an MSO in 1970 was extremely limited. In addition to small arms, the Rival had one 40 millimeter hand loaded gun on the foredeck of the ship. It utilized a four or six shell clip, shoved into the top breach of the gun by a member of the gun crew. The gun was manned when the ship was at general quarters (GQ), the highest state of readiness. When the ship was at GQ, it meant that we were on the defensive from an imminent attack. Lord help us! The gun crew was made up of the ship's only gunner's mate, and sailors who did not have any other key role to play on the ship at the time of GQ. Hence, the guys aiming and shooting the gun were not professional gunners, and kindly phrasing it, their skill always needed honing.

About every other time we went to sea for exercises, we would have gunnery practice with the 40 mm. The ship would be called to GQ, and the gun mount would be manned, awaiting a target. About that time, an empty 55 gallon oil drum would be thrown over the side of the ship, to simulate a floating mine. The lookouts would announce the sighting of this "mine," and the ship would be maneuvered into firing position. The command would be given, "Fire at will," and the gunnery crew would begin firing. Clip after clip of 40 mm shells would be loaded and fired at the floating barrel. That barrel floated quite remarkably. Either that or our crack gunnery crew kept missing. After enough frustrating time had passed and the ship needed to move on, the order would come down from the bridge for the gunner's mate to break out a rifle. The gunner's mate would then fire a few rounds from an M1 rifle, and the barrel would sink. Once again, the defense of our little ship had been expertly demonstrated.

In defense of the gun crew, remember that the ship was rocking and rolling, and the old gun mount required manual cranking by two operators to raise and lower the gun, and to adjust it side to side. By the time any adjustment could be made, the ship had rolled or moved before the gun could be fired. So it was very rare to ever hit a target in the water. But the little boy in all of us enjoyed the huge noise produced by the gun, and everyone on the ship enjoyed watching to see if that barrel would ever sink and commenting on the fantastic marksmanship skills of the gunners.

As the First Lieutenant, the Gunner's Mate and gun crew reported to me while the ship was at GQ. So while the gun was firing, I stood beside the gun and relayed orders from the bridge to the crew. In those days, we wore no ear protection, and after gunnery practice was over, I could not hear well for several hours. Today, procedures and precautions are in place to prevent the partial hearing loss that I, and many Navy gun mount crews experienced from standing next to actively firing Navy gun mounts.

Man Overboard Drills

One of the Captain and XO's favorite drills was the man overboard drill. The CO and XO especially enjoyed pulling this drill when one of the junior officers had OOD duty. The ship would be steaming along, when suddenly, the ship's intercom would blast out, "Man overboard, port (or starboard) side." The OOD would immediately need to take action to recover the man overboard. In addition, the ship's whistle was to be sounded with three long blasts to let any other ship in the vicinity know that there was a man in the water.

To simulate a man in the water, several life jackets would be tied together so that there was a visible, international orange target to re-trieve. Whichever side of the ship the man fell from, the OOD was to turn the ship in that direction. The theory was that by turning in the same direction as the falling man, the stern of the ship, where the propellers were located, would move in the opposite direction and away from the man in the water. Turning to port moved the stern to starboard, and vice versa. For example, if the man fell off the port side, the OOD was to turn to port, thereby moving the stern away from the man in the water. When the stern of the ship cleared the location of the man overboard, the OOD would then turn the ship back to starboard, and continue in a large circle until the ship came back to the same track it had originally been on, but pointed in the opposite direction to which it had been going when the man fell overboard. This turnout, followed by the complete turn back to the opposite direction is called a "Williamson turn," and is used exten-sively by ships to attempt to return to a location which they previously passed. As the OOD executed this maneuver, the CO and XO would grade the OOD on how well he performed these actions. Next, the poor OOD would have the CO and XO on the bridge watching as he at-tempted to maneuver the ship close enough to simulate picking up the man by throwing a life preserver to the man in the water. This may not sound too difficult, but add a constant wind, waves, and a rolling ship;

and the odds of cozying the ship up to the dummy in the water get much worse. If the OOD did not get close enough for the pick-up, he had to repeat the drill. The drill taught more than just procedure, though. It also allowed the OODs to practice their ship handling skills, thereby helping them become better ship drivers.

Ensign Bill

I had now been on the Rival for about eight months, was a qualified OODU, and was getting along great in my training. But my good friend LTJG Rick received official orders to another ship, and he soon left the Rival. I was sorry to see him go as he had played a large role in my training aboard the Rival. At about the same time, the ship received orders for another ensign who would soon report to the Rival. When the time came, Ensign Bill reported for duty. Bill had received his master's degree in economics, so he was very analytical and methodical. He was extremely intelligent and always seemed to be thinking about three things at once, so he often appeared to be pre-occupied.

Ensign Bill had red hair, and with his pre-occupied demeanor, he caught considerable flack from the XO and CO, with a bit of mumbling from the enlisted crew. For instance, because Bill had an advanced degree in economics, some of the crew teased him by saying such things as, "Hey Ensign Bill, did you know you wanted to go into the Navy when you majored in Home Economics?"

Bill good naturedly took it all in stride. Then his turn came for the Ensign Indoctrination from the XO and CO. I could see this one coming. As the XO and CO devised their little jokes to be played on the new ensign, I sympathized with him. As the XO and CO sent Ensign Bill on wild goose chases throughout the ship, I tried to stay out of the way and not contribute to Bill's embarrassment. I knew how he felt because I had been there, but I did not want to squelch the XO and CO's fun, for fear of getting myself in their cross hairs. Bill survived, and he was made the Supply Officer for the Rival. I moved to LTJG Rick's old job as Minesweeping Officer/First Lieutenant. I liked Bill, and we became good friends. He even moved into a little rental house across the street from us in Charleston. I recently tracked him down, and we met for lunch when he came to town for a business meeting. He's still the same great guy, just a bit older, like all of us. Another unsung hero.

Now I was pretty much where I wanted to be on the ship. I was a qualified OOD, and I was right in the midst of the action on the fantail during minesweeping exercises. I really enjoyed overseeing the operations and developed a great deal of respect for the hard working deck gang.

"Boats"

The ensign and the crusty old boatswains mate were in a bar, and they each had to use the restroom at the same time. They both attended to their business at their respective urinals. The boatswains mate finished and was just about to walk out of the restroom, when the ensign said, "At the academy, they taught us to always wash our hands after peeing." The boatswain's mate looked at the ensign a few seconds, and replied, "At boot camp twenty years ago, they taught us not to pee on our hands," and walked out.

—Author unknown

I previously mentioned Boatswain's Mate First Class Ernie, a.k.a. Boats. Boats was a crusty old guy who was probably on Noah's ark. Well, he looked the part. He was a large fellow, who chain smoked unfiltered Pall Malls. He had an outdoor ruddy complexion and a gravelly voice that rasped out orders to the deck crew. His deck crew really looked up to him as their leader, and they probably would have jumped overboard if he told them to. He and I worked very well together.

When not on duty on the ship, Ernie owned and operated a fish market in North Charleston with his wife. Jan and I would go to his market to buy fresh fish and shrimp.

As we entered the market, he would see us and shout out, "The price of fish and shrimp just went up!"

Then Jan and I would decide what we wanted to buy, and I would ask him, "How much do we owe you?"

He would get this sly smile on his old kisser and ask me, "Are you buying this, or is Mrs. Duermeyer?"

I would say, "What's the difference?"

And he would say, "For Mrs. Duermeyer, I can make a nice deal. For you, I can make another deal."

Of course he was joking that he would sell the fish cheaper to Jan, so we always said that, "Mrs. Duermeyer is buying."

Under his crusty demeanor, Ernie was a nice guy, and I really liked him. Even though I was a green young officer, he always treated me with respect and taught me all I needed to know to become a "fleet ensign," and to be his boss. That might sound odd, but in most cases, senior enlisted personnel know their jobs much better than junior officers beginning their careers. But Boats was never condescending, and we worked well as a team.

The skills of a senior boatswain's mate are many and varied. The deck crew is charged with the upkeep and constant repainting of the entire ship. In addition, the boatswain's mates are responsible for the upkeep and repair of all ground tackle on a ship. This includes all of the line and wire used on the minesweeper's gear and winches, so it was common to see one or more of the deck crew working on splicing and repairing them.

One day I was watching Boats as he weaved a new eye (permanent loop) into the end of a line. This involved taking the end of the rope, turning it back on itself, and then weaving that end into the main rope. It is a time consuming process as each main strand is weaved over and over into the main rope to ensure a strong, permanent eye. I asked him if he would teach me how to do the process. We grabbed a couple of pieces of line, and after a few minutes, he had taught me how to make a permanent eye in the rope's end. A very similar process can be used to splice two ropes end to end, and is called "bending" a rope.

Light rope line is easy to work with. But much of the ship's gear utilized cable. Working on cable to splice it, or add eyes, etc. was extremely difficult. It would sometimes take four guys to struggle with a large diameter cable to make its repairs. Unlike rope, a cable does not want to cooperate and will not bend and turn like rope. But these repairs were essential to ensure that our sweep gear could operate in a safe and efficient manner. All of our deck crew had to be taught these skills. A good boatswain's mate will also be skilled in marlinspike seamanship-the art of making special knots and decorative knots to wrap ladder railings and otherwise add decoration to ship fittings. Boats was good at this and taught his junior men how to carry on this old Navy tradition.

Remember in the "MASH" television series when Radar O'Reilley is always trading another MASH unit for something his unit needs? In the Navy, that process is call cumshaw. Another of Boats' talents was that he was a master cumshaw artist. The military slang word cumshaw means something that is obtained outside the normal supply channels, without official payment. The Navy uses this term for work that is done for a ship, usually by bartering.

One day, while I was still the supply officer on the Rival, Captain Bob told me that the ship needed a new awning for the bridge. He asked me to get to work on the project. I searched through all of my supply publications, but I could not find any reference on ordering white naugahyde for our bridge cover. I was at a loss. I knew that Boats worked miracles at times, so I went to see him.

He said, "Mr. Duermeyer, how much coffee do we have on board?"

I told him we had plenty.

He said, "C'mon, let's take a walk."

So the two of us walked down the pier and he pointed out a building we should enter. Inside, was a sail shop. Of course, the Navy no longer had sails, but the shop made special order canvas and naugahyde covers for Navy commands. Boats walked over and conferred with one of his buddies in the shop and came back over to me.

"Twenty-five pounds of coffee," he said.

We went back to the ship, and I broke out the twenty-five pounds of coffee and had it delivered to the sail shop. A week later, the ship had a brand new shiny white bridge cover. I had to be sure that we always had a large volume of coffee in the storeroom, because Boats was frequently trading with somebody for something.

Every morning, we held muster on the ship to be sure that all crew members were aboard on time, to deliver any information dealing with work for the day, and to convey any other Navy news of interest to the crew. One morning, a third class petty officer (PO), Jack, was missing from formation. After muster, I asked Boats where this individual was. Boats said he would check into it and let me know.

Later that morning, Boats pulled me aside and said, "Mr. Duermeyer, I need your help."

I said, "Sure Boats, what do you need?"

Boats then told me that PO Jack was in jail in Charleston. He had been picked up driving under the influence and speeding. He had no money, so was being held in jail pending his appearance before a judge. PO Jack was black, and the jailers, police, and judge would all be white. After all, this was the Deep South in 1969. Immediately, I had a mental picture that was not good.

Boats went on, "Mr. Duermeyer, would you consider going to court with PO Jack. He really needs a character witness, and if you go to court in uniform, the judge might go a bit easier on him."

Now, I knew PO Jack, and I also knew that he was a good worker, and we had not had any previous problems with him. So I agreed with Boats that I would go. Court was that afternoon, and after I told the XO the story, he approved our plan.

Boats and I walked into the courtroom, and sure enough, everyone in the room was white, except the defendant in the case just ahead of PO Jack's, and Jack himself. When it was PO Jack's turn, he was brought in to stand in front of the judge. The arresting police officer was there, and he told his story. The judge asked PO Jack if what the officer had said was true. PO Jack affirmed that it was true, but apologized for his actions. The judge then asked the court room if there was anyone who could vouch for the defendant. I raised my hand. The judge asked me to come forward. I stepped up to the bench and told the judge that I was PO Jack's department head on the ship, and that we needed PO Jack because we were short-handed. In addition, I told the judge that PO Jack was a hard worker, and that I felt that he had learned his lesson and would probably never do this again. The judge looked at me and smirked.

"$500 and no jail time! Mr. Jack, I better never see you in this court room again. Next case," said the judge.

I wasn't sure what just happened, but I tend to think that because Ernie and I were in court, the judge did not put PO Jack back in jail. For that we were grateful. But, PO Jack did not have $500. Boats and I huddled, and I then asked the judge if we could bring in the money later this afternoon. The judge agreed, but PO Jack would return to jail until the money was paid. Boats and I hot-footed it back to the ship, and I left Ernie while he was rounding up the deck crew. In a few minutes, Ernie came to see me and asked to leave the ship for a while. I agreed. I knew what was going on. Ernie had asked for donations from his crew to get PO Jack out of jail.

Later, Ernie returned to the ship with PO Jack in tow. PO Jack came over and told me that he appreciated my efforts on his behalf. After that, the price of my fish and shrimp purchases went down a bit at Ernie's market. That's the kind of guy Ernie (Boats) was. He was one of my special unsung heroes.

Ship Yard

Sometime in the fall of 1969, the Rival was ordered into the ship yards in Jacksonville, Florida. The primary reason for a minesweeper to go into the yards was to recondition the outer hull of the ship. The wooden hulls tended to deteriorate faster in salt water. In addition, if the wooden ship was ported in warm tropical waters, it was notoriously a magnet for attracting water-borne ship worms that would literally eat the oak planking. So the ships periodically went into the shipyards for hull work.

The Rival traveled to Jacksonville, Florida, and met the shipyard tugs outside the dry dock. Ever so slowly, the ship was moved into the floating dry dock and was centered in the dry dock in preparation for the dry dock to be raised. Divers then went under the ship and placed huge blocks on which the ship would rest when it was in the dry dock. The water in the dry dock was then pumped out, and the dry dock slowly rose with the Rival snugly ensconced. The ship soon sat high and dry within the dry dock.

The Rival was in the yards for four to six weeks, during which time the hull was reconditioned, and other minor repairs were made to the ship. I was fascinated with the mechanics of how a large, heavy ship could be taken out of the water and placed on blocks. On numerous occasions, I went to the bottom of the dry dock and walked beneath the ship to watch the shipyard workers as they worked on the hull. Some adjustments were also made to the ship's screws, and the screw hubs were disassembled, revealing the inner hub gears. I could then see how those variable pitch propellers actually worked. The drawback to being in the shipyard was that we continued to live on the ship while it was crawling with workers, and while the cacophony of noise reverberated throughout the ship. Everything was covered with a layer of grit and dirt, which permeated the air during the sandblasting of the hull. The less than perfect living arrangements on the ship certainly got worse.

A Navy man walks into a bar, gives the bartender a conspiratorial wink, and says, "Quick, pour me a drink before the trouble starts." The bartender pours a drink and watches as the sailor downs it in one gulp. The sailor slams the glass down on the bar and says, "Quick, give me another one before the trouble starts." The bartender pours another glass and the sailor drinks it just as fast as the previous one. The sailor lets out a belch, and demands another drink before the trouble starts. After a couple more rounds of this, the bartender says, "Look sailor, you've been talking about trouble for ten minutes. Just when is this trouble going to start?" The sailor looks at the bartender, grins, and says, "The trouble starts just as soon as you find out I don't have any money."

—Author unknown

On many evenings, those junior officers who did not have the duty on the ship would frequent a little burger and beer dive right outside the gate of the shipyard. At least it was a short respite from the monotony, noise, and gritty dirt on the ship.

One evening when I was in that dive by myself, nursing a beer, the middle-aged woman who was tending the bar spoke to me.

She said, "Do all you Navy Officers keep your wedding rings on when you go into a bar?"

I was wearing mine at the time. I thought for a minute and knew what she was implying.

I responded, "I guess those who are happily married keep theirs on."

She just grinned and said, "Well, if you want to take that ring off some time, just let me know."

Yeah right, like that was going to happen. After that, I always went in that joint with another junior officer.

Our shipyard period finally came to a close, and the Rival looked much better. A considerable amount of her hull sheathing had been replaced, and she was freshly painted and looked as good as new. We then left the yard and headed back to Charleston, where we continued our local operations and training.

The Drawdown

At the end of 1969, I had been on the Rival nine months. I was getting along great in my job, and I had earned the respect of the crew, and the CO and XO. I was content with my position. But at the end of the year, we began hearing rumors that the Mine Force ships were going to be cut back in number. Sure enough, the Rival and several other MSOs received word that they would be going through a decommissioning process. The ship would either be mothballed or sold as scrap, even though the ship had just recently completed an extensive, and undoubtedly expensive overhaul in the shipyard.

For people who work in private industry, this was like being told that your company was closing. The morale on the ship instantly took a big dive. The Rival would now go through a long, drawn-out process to put the ship out of commission. All salvageable equipment that could be used by other ships in the Navy would have to be removed from the ship, and slowly but surely, the ship would go through a huge list of procedures to literally seal up the ship so that it could be towed to a Navy mothball fleet location.

The biggest question on the minds of each individual crew member was, "I wonder what will happen to me." Naturally, I had the same question. I found out rather quickly. First of all, the ship would never again go to sea with its full crew. We would remain in port and begin the complicated decommissioning procedures. Shortly thereafter, LTJG Ken received official orders to report to another ship. Now there were three junior officers, and we would now be standing one-in-three in port watches. That meant that we would stay aboard the ship every third night while the ship was in port. Not long after that, ENS Bill received his orders. So, LTJG Ben and I were now standing "port and starboard," meaning every other night, one of us had the duty. But wait, it gets worse. LTJG Ben also received orders to leave the ship. Now, I was the only junior officer on the ship as it continued the decommissioning process. That meant that as the only junior officer, I was standing "port and port." I had to be on the ship every night, and of course, every day. I could not leave the ship. After a few nights of this, I pleaded with the XO to see how we could change this situation. To my relief, with the CO's permission, the XO himself volunteered to stand duty watches. So he and I alternated the nights we remained on board. Even having to stand port and starboard was better than being on the ship around the clock every day.

In February, I completed my first year in the Navy as an Ensign, and was promoted to Lieutenant Junior Grade (LTJG). This helped our family budget, of course, but also made me very proud to wear my new silver rank insignia. At about the same time, I also received orders to go to another ship. I was ordered to the USS Pinnacle (MSO-462). I was disappointed, because I was going to another MSO, and it was merely a matter of walking over to the next pier and reporting aboard. I would rather have moved to a different type of ship, where I would have gained additional experience and perhaps been able to travel more. But in March 1970, I reported to the Pinnacle.

USS Pinnacle (MSO-462)[13]

The Pinnacle's career[14]

Laid down	August 24, 1953
Launched	January 3, 1955
Commissioned	October 21, 1955
Decommissioned	1971
Struck from Navy roles	November 1, 1977
Homeport	Charleston, SC
Fate	Sold for scrap May 1, 1978

---

[13] NAVSOURCE Naval History—Photographic History of the U.S. Navy, http://www. NAVSOURCE.org/archives/11/02462.htm.

[14] Ibid.

The Pinnacle's characteristics[15]

Displacement	775 tons
Length	172 feet
Beam	35 feet
Draught	10 feet
Top Speed	14 knots
Complement	6 Officers 74 Enlisted
Armament	One 40 mm mount
Propulsion	4 Packard ID 1700 diesel engines, Twin screw, variable pitch propellers

The USS Pinnacle (MSO-462)

Physically, the Pinnacle was virtually the same as the Rival. The only big difference was that the Pinnacle had Packard Diesel engines, versus the Rival's Waukasha diesels.

My assignment on the Pinnacle was First Lieutenant, and later Operations Department Head. To become qualified for the operations position, the Navy sent me to a couple more schools in Charleston. Specifically, I attended a security course and a cryptology course. These courses would enable me to receive classified documents, publications, and to decode encrypted messages. When the ship went to sea, I spent a great deal of time in the radio room, where our ship's message traffic was received and where my classified vault was located, and in the Combat Information Center (CIC) plotting our ship's course in relation to our exercises. I enjoyed this work, and it was a real change from first lieutenant job on the Rival. I also had a good friend in the radio crew. Our radioman first class petty officer, called "Schmutzie," was one of the most impressive sailors I ever met. He was always "squared away." His uniform was always clean and pressed, and he could have posed for a Navy recruiting poster. He knew his job backwards and forwards and was always a huge help to me in the operations department. He is another of the many unsung heroes that I met along the way in my Navy days, and I often wonder what happened to this fine young man.

As in private industry, from company to company, the "management" of a Navy ship can vary from ship to ship. By ship's management, I mean the CO, XO, the junior officers, and the leading petty officers. The Pinnacle CO and XO were very different from the Rival. For me, my

---

[15] Ibid.

time on the Pinnacle was not very enjoyable. As soon as I came onboard the Pinnacle, it was apparent that the crew morale was poor. The biggest contributing factor was that the future of the Charleston minesweeping fleet was a real unknown. The MSO force had been cut in half with many of the ships sitting at the pier preparing for decommissioning and moth-balling. No one at the ship level knew what would happen to the rest of the ships. Sailors generally take a great deal of pride in the ship on which they serve, and they want to do their very best to make their ship a suc-cess. But I did not get this feeling from the crew of the Pinnacle. We did not know if we were just spinning our wheels waiting for the decommis-sioning orders or whether the Pinnacle was a bona fide player in the Navy's arsenal. To make matters worse, the CO of the Pinnacle was somewhat aloof and unapproachable, so was not very well liked by the crew. He may have come from a larger ship or a staff position where this behavior was the norm. But on a small ship, where everyone bumps into each other, literally and figuratively all day long, the entire crew gets very familiar with each other, and the atmosphere is much more infor-mal. Now a LTJG, I was second most senior of the four junior officers on the Pinnacle. As such, the enlisted men knew they could approach me with questions or concerns, and I would listen to them and try to help them when I could. Many of the men were younger than I was, and they often came to me, asking for my opinion on matters in their professional and private lives. In OCS I had been taught that officers should be a source for counseling and guidance for the enlisted men, and I enjoyed these talks. I always thought this relationship with the crew was a good thing, but the CO did not. He thought I was far too close to the enlisted crew.

An example was the close working relationship I had with the ship's leading radioman, RMI Schmutzie. We laughed and joked with each oth-er, but always retained the Officer/Enlisted boundaries. One day the CO came in the radio room where Schmutzie and I were laughing over a joke while sorting the radio traffic. Later that day the CO admonished me again about being too friendly with the enlisted members of the crew.

The CO was Navy old school. But the Navy was rapidly changing and breaking down some of the old protocol. The leader in making these changes in the Navy was the Chief of Naval Operations (CNO) at the time, Admiral Elmo Zumwalt. Admiral Zumwalt made so many changes, and so fast, that some of the old Navy officers did not like him, nor did they like some of his more progressive orders from Washington to the fleet. The Navy was becoming younger oriented with the typical sailor being much smarter and more technically savvy than before. Admiral Zumwalt was aware of this, and I believe his intent was to bring the

Navy and Navy personnel into this new, more technical environment. But some Navy COs, including the CO of the Pinnacle tended to drag their feet at some of the CNO's changes.

The "Z-Grams"

> *Little Johnnie asked his mother, "Momma, don't sailors ever go to heaven?" "Of course they do," said his mother. "Why do you ask?" Johnnie said, "There are so many sailors with beards, but I never saw any pictures of angels with beards." His mother answered, "Oh, that's because most men who go to heaven get there by a close shave."*
>
> —*Author unknown*

At the height of his tenure as CNO, Admiral Zumwalt's office sent messages to all Navy commands at a dizzying, blizzard rate.[16] Sometimes it seemed there would be two or three messages per day. The Navy fleet had nicknamed all of this message traffic from the CNO as, "Z-Grams." Often the COs in the fleet would shudder when a new Z-Gram was received, because most of the Z-Grams would affect the autonomy of the COs in how they operated their respective ships. Some of these messages made small changes in the way the Navy operated, but many of them concerned changes being made in an to attempt to lift the morale of the enlisted sailor.

A copy of the Z-Grams that affected the enlisted sailors was always posted on the bulletin board in the enlisted dining area (mess deck), so that the crew could all see the latest news from CNO. All of this Navy policy-making was way above my pay grade, so although I read the messages with interest, they really did not affect me that much. My job was to receive the messages in our communications area and then quickly route the message traffic to the CO, XO, and all officers. But one day, I was affected.

On this particular day, a new Z-Gram had been received. In this message, the CNO had authorized all sailors to wear sideburns, mustaches, and beards if they chose to. The message was routed as usual, a copy was posted on the mess deck for the crew, and I thought nothing more about it. But later in the day, while the noon meal was being served to the crew, I happened to walk through the mess deck area by the bulletin board. The

---

[16] Naval Historical Center, Washington, D.C., Frequently Asked Questions, Z-grams— Policy Directives Issued by Admiral Zumwalt While in Office as Chief of Naval Operations, 1 July 1970-1 July 1974, http://www.history.navy.mil/faqs/faq93-2.htm.

bulletin board was at the base of a ladder leading to the next higher deck, where the Captain's cabin was located.

As I was walking through the mess deck, several members of the crew corralled me and asked point blank, "Mr. Duermeyer, do you think the Captain will allow us to grow beards and sideburns?"

They knew the nature of the CO, and they were unsure whether the Captain would carry out the directive from CNO. This put me in an awkward position. I wanted to be fair to the crew, but I also did not want to denigrate the authority of my CO. I walked over to the bulletin board and began reading the specific Z-Gram out loud.

After reading the directive, I said to the crew, "From what I read here, I don't really see how the CO cannot comply with the directive. I would say that he had to allow the beards and sideburns."

Suddenly, from above me up the ladder I heard, "Mr. Duermeyer!" Oh crap, it was the Captain's voice. "Mr. Duermeyer, come to my cabin, now!"

I climbed the ladder and entered the CO's cabin. He sat at his desk glaring at me, and told me to close the door. And then the scalding began.

"Mr. Duermeyer, I am the Commanding Officer of this ship. As such, I am responsible for everything that goes on anywhere on this ship. Nothing can be done on this ship without my permission. Who in the hell do you think you are that you can tell the crew what policy will be on my ship? I don't care what messages may say that come to this ship, because I will interpret them and make the policy decisions for this ship. Furthermore, there will be no sideburns or beards on this ship while I am the Commanding Officer!"

It went on much longer than this, but you get the idea. No slimy little LTJG was going to interpret message traffic from the CNO for the crew without having the CO's blessing. This dust up between the CO and me was an indicator of the working relationship I would always have with that CO. I was always respectful to him, I always carried out my orders to the best of my ability, and I did an excellent job as the Operations Department Head. But the CO just did not bond with his junior officers, and that was certainly true in my case. As I said before, there were good COs and not so great COs in the Navy, and I was serving under one for whom I really had very little respect. And the crew's respect for him was reflected in the morale of the men. It probably could not be said that the CO of the Pinnacle and I had a mutual admiration society.

Even though it meant attempting to disregard the orders of the CNO, true to his word, the CO banned beards and sideburns on the Pinnacle. The crew took another dip in morale, especially after they saw other sailors on the base sporting their new beards and sideburns. But as part of the Admiral Zumwalt policy changes, the Admiral also set up an ombudsman office, which any sailor could call if he had problems in his Navy career. Well, you can predict what happened, of course. A couple weeks elapsed, and the word was quietly and unceremoniously put out by the XO at quarters one morning that the crew would now be allowed to wear beards and grow sideburns. It was very likely that some member of the crew had ratted out the CO. I can truthfully say that it was not me, but you can certainly surmise how I felt.

It was impossible to ignore a directive from the CNO, even if you were the CO of a ship. Unfortunately, this whole incident may have added to the CO's dislike for me. He still felt I took up the cause for the enlisted guys far too often.

The morale on board the Pinnacle was also reflected in the wardroom. The officers were not nearly as "tight" as we had been on the Rival. On the Rival, we had liked and respected one another. On the Pinnacle, this was not the case. We each just wanted to do our jobs and get the heck off the ship.

Meal time in the wardroom was also not the same as it had been on the Rival. Generally at meals, the officers would tell stories and laugh at each other and joke around. Otherwise, we would discuss pending operations and/or procedures that the ship would be undergoing. In other words, business and humor would be the norm. But on the Pinnacle, the flow of conversation was never very free-wheeling, and was not especially pleasant. The meal time conversation tended to be uni-directional, if you get my drift. Additionally, we all were simply waiting to see if the Pinnacle would survive future mine force cuts.

The Minesweeper Sailor's Constant Concern

Fire aboard an MSO was a constant concern and worry for the whole crew. Being a wooden ship, fire safety onboard was a huge priority. During the era of the wooden MSOs serving in the world-wide Navy's fleets, six MSOs were destroyed by fire.[17] Precautions were always taken whenever there was any open flame for welding or brazing, and in some cases if the risk was high, a charged fire hose watch stood by while the activity was taking place. In addition, when the ship was in port, the OOD would hold a fire drill onboard every night. Sometimes an OOD would even start a small paper fire in a metal garbage can to let the watch section actually put out a small fire. Egad, what were we thinking?

---

[17] *Conway's All the World's Fighting Ships, 1947-1982*, Conway Maritime Press Ltd., 1983.

One night while in port, the unthinkable happened to another ship. One of the other MSOs that was tied farther down the pier from us caught fire. The fire built fast, and soon it was raging through the ship. The crew was trying their best to extinguish the fires, but they were losing the fight to the fire. With all the fire hoses putting water on the fire, the ship was also taking on water at a high rate.

Soon the Naval base fire department trucks came roaring down the pier to assist, adding their fire equipment and water to the fire fight. Now, the ship was taking on a great deal more water, and the ship was slowly lowering in the water.

Finally the base fire chief yelled at the ship's crew, "Do you have your evacuation pumps running?" (The evacuation pumps would pump water out of the ship and send it overboard.)

The MSO crew replied that the pumps were running at the maximum setting. The ship's crew and the fire department continued pouring water on the fire, and the ship kept sinking even lower in the water. The ship was literally sinking at the pier! As the fire slowly was brought under control, the fire chief asked the ship's crew to check on the evacuation pumps again. Ship's personnel were sent below. They returned to sheepishly tell the OOD on deck that the evacuation pumps were working properly, but that a sea valve had been reversed, so instead of pumping water off the ship, the pumps were bringing sea water into the ship. That certainly explained the ship's rapid sinking at the pier! The final result of the horrible episode was that the ship was damaged beyond repair and was a total loss.

In my research and memory, I could not find the name of the ship to which this incident occurred in Charleston. Imagine almost burning to the water line and nearly sinking at the pier. Remember that whatever happens to a Navy ship, the Captain is always ultimately responsible. So, unfortunately, the CO of that ship would be facing some serious consequences for losing his ship. Thank goodness it was not the Pinnacle that had this extremely unfortunate experience.

Another Drawdown

The Pinnacle continued to carry out local operations and exercises at sea through 1970. As long as the crew stayed busy and the ship was operating, morale stayed up. But word was soon received that more of the Charleston MSO fleet was going to be cut. Sure enough, Pinnacle was named for decommissioning and mothballing. I was going to go through this same nightmare again along with many of the sailors who had also gone through a previous decommissioning. When word was received of Pinnacle's fate, everyone wanted to vacate the ship as quickly as possible. Our ship was of no further use to the Navy, and none of us wanted to be under that cloud any more. The crew pitched in and quickly completed all of the tasks to make the ship ready for decommissioning. The faster we could accomplish this, the faster we could get on with moving to another command.

Along with all this work, a great deal of the day was spent with sailors and officers calling their Washington detailers trying to bug the detailers into cutting a new set of orders to get off the ship. I was no exception. I wanted off the Pinnacle, the sooner the better.

Once again I asked for advice from my savvy brother, Steve. I called him and asked what he thought would be the best move I could make to further my Navy career. I told him I was thoroughly fed up with minesweeper duty. I felt it was fruitless duty with no excitement, and I wanted an assignment where I could excel and grow professionally. He said that I needed to get a Department Head job on a larger ship or an XO's job on a small ship. Either one of these positions would be an aid to promotion and enhancing my career.

I spent hours on the phone to Washington trying to get through to my particular detailer. When I finally reached him, I told him that I wanted a job in which I would be challenged and one in which I could grow. We agreed that an XO billet would be the way to go, and I asked the detailer to find one of those jobs for me, if possible. Another week went by, and I called Washington again. I reached the detailer, and he gave me the good news. There was an XO billet available out of Pearl Harbor, on the USS Ute (ATF-76). An ATF is an ocean-going fleet salvage tug. It had six officers and eighty enlisted personnel. Wow, Hawaii! The detailer then told me there was a caveat to taking the XO billet. I would have to extend my contracted military obligation for another six months in addition to the year I presently had left on my obligation. At this point, I was still intending to make the Navy a lifetime career, so the extra six month obligation was immaterial to me, and I agreed to the extension.

The detailer and I continued our discussion, and I asked, "Is the ship doing duty in Vietnam?"

The detailer replied affirmatively. My stomach flipped. Deep inside, this is what I wanted. I wanted to move toward involvement in the Vietnam war, but reality sort of sneaks up on me sometimes. Another reality was that the Ute was a real steamer. That meant that it was deployed every year for six months. That would be a lot of time away from Janet and Hawaii. I swallowed and told the detailer the XO job was just what I wanted. The detailer would send me orders as soon as possible.

After a few days of thinking about the situation and many discussions with Janet, I got more and more psyched up about the XO job. Officers in the Navy who have served on board ships and COs of Navy ships always say, "If you can do a shipboard XO's job, you can do any job in the Navy." The XO's job is extremely tough, demanding, and affords an officer the opportunity to learn even more about command at sea by working closely with the ship's CO. I was worried about my ability, yet excited about fulfilling this demanding role on a ship at sea. I was thrilled that I was about to leave the Pinnacle and would soon see a lot more of the world under action conditions. A new, exciting chapter in my life would soon begin.

In November 1970, I received my orders to report to the USS Ute (ATF-76). I was granted some leave, and after the movers came for our personal belongings in Charleston, Jan and I headed to Iowa for a visit with our parents. We had learned that for families that had pets, arrival in Hawaii required that the family pet would be placed in quarantine for several months. We did not want to subject Heidi to that, so we found her a new home with some friends in Charleston before we left. We would sure miss her later.

We packed everything we were taking with us into our little baby blue Volkswagen bug. It was loaded down. The poor little bug struggled through the Smoky Mountains, sometimes even in second gear as we headed north for Iowa. We spent a great time with the families, and soon it was time for continuing our trek to the West Coast. Once again the little blue VW bug struggled with all its might to cross the Rockies as we headed to California. At this point I had had it with a car that spent so much time in second gear struggling up hills. So when we arrived in San Diego, we visited a Chevy dealer on the famous San Diego "Mile of Cars" and traded for a Chevrolet Nova, a much nicer and larger car. We stayed in San Diego while I attended a prospective XO school. The school was intended to teach an overview of the rudiments of carrying out the duties of a ship's executive officer. In addition, I took a refresher course on the proper care and handling of classified documents.

Jan and I stayed in a low-rent, furnished apartment while in San Diego. We still laugh about that shabby place. But even funnier, the apartment house was built around an open courtyard. All of the apartments faced the courtyard. Across the courtyard lived an older couple, who were the managers of this wholesome abode, and coincidentally who were probably both certified alcoholics. In the evenings, especially, they would get wound up in the sauce, and start loudly yelling and cursing each other. These spats would go on for hours until they finally ran out of steam. There were many nights in that place when we missed out on our sleep.

Finally, the San Diego courses were completed, and we again loaded the car, this time headed for San Francisco for more Navy schools. We were driving, of course, and as we passed through Los Angeles we had our first experience with the famous Los Angeles urban smog. Not just any smog, but greenish yellow smog so thick you could cut it with a knife. Remember, this was 1971. Our eyes burned so bad that I could not see to drive and had to exit the freeway. We splashed water on our eyes and continued north. We wondered how the LA natives could survive in that pollution. Although the area still has smog, the atmosphere in southern California is considerably clearer today.

As part of my job as the XO on the Ute, I was to be the ship's navigator. Remember my struggle in OCS with navigation? How is that for irony? Frankly, the prospect of becoming a ship's navigator, who is held accountable for knowing the location of the ship at all times, had me a bit worried.

We arrived in San Francisco and found a place to stay while I attended Navigation School on Treasure Island. Treasure Island no longer belongs to the Navy, but at that time it was a major Navy Training Command with many different Navy schools on the island. With impending doom, I started my first day of navigation school. But what a surprise; I had no difficulty handling the course and did very well in my studies. Apparently, it was all in the presentation. The Treasure Island course was taught by a Senior Quartermaster Chief, and I believe he taught in a more rote procedural manner. In this way, I could grasp the processes and got along fine.

With the schools behind me, it was time to continue westward. Jan and I checked our car into the freight movers who would transport it to Hawaii, and we flew out of San Francisco headed for Honolulu. In Honolulu there would be Navy quarters for us, but we were placed on a waiting list for a few weeks. This meant that Jan would be in temporary housing for a while. In the meantime, the Ute was in the Philippine Islands (PI), and I would need to fly there to meet the ship. A week or so later a flight was arranged for me, and I would fly to the PI. I kissed my sweetie good-by at the base flight terminal where I would catch the flight.

Prior to my departure, I was to report to medical for a review of my records before going overseas. I waited while the doctors reviewed my records, and then I heard, "Mr. Duermeyer." Oh crap, now what? "Please report to Inoculation." Ugh, even worse. It turned out that I was missing a few mandatory shots for overseas duty. So, like a good sailor, I bared the appropriate dermal areas and was given four shots, including yellow fever, typhoid, and the highly ill-rumored gamma globulin shot. With that unpleasantness behind me, I was ready to board the plane leaving Honolulu, headed for Manila, PI.

In those days, the Navy had an additional officers' uniform, which is no longer used. You will see it on the old Navy Hollywood World War II movies. It is a khaki wool, dress uniform with shirt and tie, slacks, and a gold buttoned suit coat with shoulder boards. I was wearing this very warm, but required, uniform on the plane as we winged west.

About two hours into the flight, the side effects of the shots kicked in. I became feverish, sweating profusely, and my back side felt like a horse had kicked it. I was in misery. The stewardess (sorry, that's what they were called at that time) noticed my condition and brought me some cold orange juice.

She said, "I wish they would give you overseas guys a couple days to get over these shots before you have to fly."

Apparently this shot syndrome was nothing new to her. The orange juice only added to the equation, and an upset stomach became part of my list of discomforts. This went on for hours. The flight to Manila was many hours, and the side effects of the shots finally subsided shortly before we landed. By that time, I was totally wiped out. I had not eaten anything, nor had I slept in over twenty four hours.

A Navy bus picked up Navy passengers at the Manila airport and hauled us to the huge Subic Bay Naval Base on the island of Luzon. I reported to the base OOD and asked at which pier the Ute was berthed. I was told the Ute was at sea, and I would have to find a room at the Bachelor Officers' Quarters (BOQ). I found a base taxi and went to the BOQ, only to find out that they had no space. But they called around and found out that Clark Air Force Base had room. Clark was quite a distance from the Navy base, and I took a military shuttle bus to Clark. I was dropped off at the BOQ and given a key to a room. When I got there, I discovered that the room was actually a trailer with two rooms, each with three bunks. My roommates for the night would be other junior officers in transit; both Navy and Air Force. I took a quick shower, crashed on a bunk, and attempted to sleep.

Another First

In the BOQ area, there was a lot of noise, with officers coming and going and many of them coming back to quarters after having been out on the town having a good time. I tossed and turned in my strange, noisy surroundings, and finally managed to doze off. But then, about three a.m., I was awakened to a banging sound, and the flimsy trailer we were sleeping in was literally shaking. In my half-sleep, I thought the guy in the next room must have brought a girlfriend home with him. The banging and shaking went on for a long time. Once again, I tried and managed to doze off. In the morning, all of my roommates asked me how I liked the earthquake last night. Earthquake? I had never experienced an earthquake before. So that was the source of the banging and shaking during the night. I felt a bit foolish for my personal assessment of the previous night's activity. This would not be the last time I had earthquake encounters. Years later, while living in southern California, Jan and I experienced many earthquakes.

The Ute was to return to the Navy base the next day, and I caught a bus to head back there too. The temperature must have been one hundred degrees with a humidity reading to match, and I still had on the same wool uniform in which I had traveled.

When I arrived at the pier and stepped off the bus, I stood and looked at the Ute for a few moments. This was going to be my new home, and it had to be one of the pug-ugliest little ships I had ever seen. It hit me again, then, that I was going to be the Executive Officer of this little ship, and my stomach started doing flip flops as I made my way up the brow of the ship, saluted the ensign (flag), and asked for directions to the CO's cabin.

Part Three

Navy Auxiliary Ships

THE Ute was a Navy auxiliary ship. As I mentioned before, Navy sailors who have served onboard auxiliary ships refer to these ships as "the working Navy." The ships receive no glory and are not considered the glamour ships. They are not generally in combat. Instead, they fulfill numerous roles in support of the combat ships and other Naval operational units. The work on these ships is extremely hard and dangerous. There is always a great deal of pure physical, dirty work for the sailors, and in the course of a work day on an auxiliary, sailors earn a coat of dirt and grime while carrying out their duties. Hence, this group of hard working sailors consider themselves to be part of the working Navy, and tend to, a bit scornfully, consider sailors on non-auxiliaries to have "cushy," non-physical jobs.

Without the auxiliaries, the primary Navy combatants cannot carry out sustained operations at sea. In addition, the auxiliaries replenish ground operations by bringing essential cargo to the theater of operations for use by both ground and sea units participating in that theater. For those Navy units in need of repair, and which also may need salvage operations, the auxiliaries provide that assistance as well. To carry out these missions, there are numerous types of ships falling into the auxiliary class of ships. Most of the ships' roles will fit into replenishment, transport, repair, harbor craft, or research.

The following table shows some of the classifications and the purposes of those ships.[18,19] The table is not all-inclusive, as the Navy operates many other auxiliaries in addition to those listed. The table serves as illustration only, to show the wide diversity of the ships, and some of the types of jobs entrusted to the auxiliaries.

Role	Hull Designation
Replenishment. Direct support of Navy units by providing either underway or shore offloading of fuel, ammunition, food, and supplies of other necessities for afloat or shore based front line units	AE—ammunition ship AF/AFS—combat stores ship (food) AO/AOE—fuel tankers and combination fuel and ammo
Transport. Support of forward units	AK/AKA/AKL/AKS—cargo

[18] List of Auxiliaries of the United States Navy, Wikipedia, http://en.www.wikipedia.org/wiki/List_of_Auxiliaries_of_the_United_States_Navy.
[19] U.S. Navy Auxiliary Ships' Pictures, http://BLUEJACKET.com/usn_ship_image_ad-ah.html.

by transporting supplies needed at the theater, as well as underway replenishment or offloading to shore	ships AP/APA/APB—transport ships
Repair ships. Ships that provide full repair services and overhaul capabilities to front line ships	AR—general repair ships ARD and ARL—large and small repair ships ARS—Salvage ships, also capable of towing vessels ASR—diving and salvage ship ATF—fleet ocean tugs, also capable of salvage work AS—submarine repair ship AD—destroyer/cruiser repair ship
Harbor Craft. Small boats which work usually within the harbor, providing services to larger Navy units	Yard tugs, yard oilers, water craft, cranes, and other small support craft fall into this category.
Research ships. Provide the Navy with data regarding operating environment or assisting with testing of new technology.	AG/AGB/AGS—Used for oceanic survey work. Many of these ships were also manned by commercial research companies or entities. They also could see duty in missile tracking or as command ships.
Medical ships. I have added this separate category to include the tremendous, unique support provided by hospital ships at a theater of operations.	AH—hospital ship. Two such ships, the Repose, and the Sanctuary served in Vietnam. Anchored or cruising off the coast, they provided state of the art medical facilities to injured front line warriors, thereby saving thousands of lives.

The Ute was an ATF, a fleet ocean-going tug. ATFs were extremely powerful little ships. As a point of illustration, ATFs were so powerful, that it was said that an ATF could tow an aircraft carrier, many times larger than an ATF. In reality, if an aircraft carrier were in need of a tow, it is more likely that it would be accomplished by a team of tugs. In addition, an ATF carried assorted salvage gear, primarily used for pulling other ships off of a location where the other ship had been grounded by accident or weather. ATFs saw a great deal of action in salvage operations during World War II and the Korean War. Armed with a three-inch gun mount, they also participated in shore bombardment in these two wars[20]

---

[20] Dictionary of American Naval Fighting Ships, Department of the Navy, http://www.history.navy.mil/danfs/u2/ute.htm.

Officer Candidate James Duermeyer standing watch at Nimitz Hall, Officer Candidate School, Newport, R.I. 1968.

USS Rival (MSO-468) being refueled at sea (date unknown).

Ensign Duermeyer standing on the pilot house weather deck to the right of the Rival nameplate, with Boatswain's Mate Ernie standing on the main deck, lower right as the Rival returns from sea. 1969.

Wardroom of the USS Pinnacle at the Pinnacle's decommissioning ceremony. LTJG Duermeyer is on the far right and the CO of the Pinnacle is in the center of the group. 1970.

USS Pinnacle (MSO-462) underway at sea. Date unknown.

USS Ute (ATF-76) underway at sea. Date unknown.

Going . . . .

Going . . . .

Gone—and ready to start again.

These photos taken from another Navy ship show the typical ride at sea of the USS Ute while underway in WESTPAC going into the waves. The first shot shows the bow of the Ute completely above the surface of the sea. The second shot shows the bow entering the water again, and the third shot shows the bow of the ship submerged. This was very typical of the type of roller-coaster ride of the little ship. I was unable to find the original source of these pictures. I believe they may have appeared in *All Hands Magazine* nearly forty years ago, but I was unable to find these pictures in a search of that magazine's archives.

LT James Duermeyer, executive officer and navigator of the USS Ute (ATF-76). 1972.

LTJG James Duermeyer and Janet Duermeyer prior to attending a Navy party. 1971.

LT Duermeyer on morning inspection rounds in the Chief's Quarters on the USS Ute (ATF-76). 1972.

Left to right, Ens. Adam, LTJG Duermeyer, and LTJG Pat on the wing of the bridge of the USS Ute (ATF-76). 1971.

.50 caliber gunnery practice on the starboard bridge wing mount on the USS Ute (ATF-76) This picture was taken the same day one of our sailors was injured by a misfire of the .50 caliber. 1971.

A view from the stern of the USS Ute (ATF-76) showing a three ship tow from Vietnam to Subic Bay – a yard water craft, a yard oiler, and an MSO. 1971.

USS Ute (ATF-76) towing a floating crane, similar to the crane that broke away from the Ute and had to be chased and re-rigged for towing to Subic. 1971.

A crowded street scene in Alongapo, P.I. showing a line of Jeepneys waiting to pick up passengers. 1971.

Young boys who dive for coins in the polluted river under the bridge leading from the Subic Bay Navy base into Alongapo P.I. 1971.

A South Vietnamese coastal patrol boat passes across the bow of the USS Ute (ATF-76) while she is at anchor in Vietnamese waters. 1971.

The rugged, but beautiful shoreline of Grande Island, P.I., a favorite place for the Ute crew to go diving and snorkeling. 1971.

Security watch on the bow of the Ute while at anchor in Vietnamese waters. They were to watch for unauthorized swimmers approaching the ship.

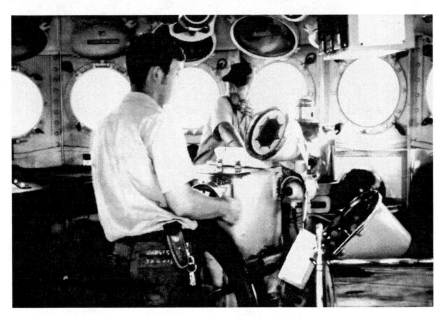

The helmsman is steering the Ute while watching his gyro compass and engine order telegraph. The Quartermaster of the Watch is standing at the front of the pilot house of the USS Ute (ATF-76). 1971.

The USS Ute (ATF-76) returning from a WESTPAC cruise wearing the flower lei handmade by the ship's wives' club. 1971.

Left to right Warrant Officer Cobie, Captain Archie, and LTJG Duermeyer standing at the rail of the Ute as she is moored to the dock after returning from
WESTPAC 1971.

One of the Indonesian gunboats tied up to the pier at Midway Island for refueling. It is one of the three gun boats that the Ute accompanied/towed from Pearl
Harbor to Surabaya, Indonesia. 1972.

The Indonesian Commodore's gunboat, traveling on its own power as it continues its journey to Surabaya. 1972.

The slimy pollywogs are gathered on the forecastle of the Ute to be washed down with fire hoses to wash of their slime. 1972.

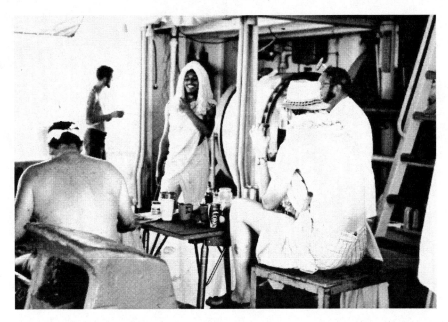

Davey Jones in his straw hat, the Royal Baby on the left, and the Royal Queen (with the mop on the head) await the sentencing of the next pollywog during crossing the equator ceremonies. 1972.

LT Duermeyer, Executive Officer of the USS Ute (ATF-76) after kissing the royal baby several times in his initiation to become a trusty shellbacks. 1972.

The Ute passes these deteriorating combatant ships in the Surabaya, Indonesia harbor as it enters Surabaya. At the time, Indonesia was purchasing used combatant ships from Russia or China. 1972.

The Ute at anchor in Hong Kong harbor, with a U.S. Navy submarine moored to the Ute. 1972.

Primo, the ship's dog, at his usual place, standing watch with his buddies on the quarterdeck while the Ute is in port. 1971.

The Ute's rock and roll band singing in the Crazy Horse Bar in Hong Kong. LTJG Duermeyer with the microphone. 1971.

LTJG James Duermeyer. 1971.

Part Four

USS Ute (ATF-76)

The Ute (ATF-76)

USS Ute (ATF-76)[21]

The Ute's career[22]

Laid down	February 27, 1942
Launched	June 24, 1942
Commissioned	December 13, 1942
Ute was transferred to the *Military Transportation Service*	Approximately 1974 to 1979 as USNS Ute
Placed out of service and transferred to the US Coast Guard	Served approximately eight years as USCGC Ute
Final decommissioning	May 26 1988
Fate	Sunk as a target August 4, 1999

The Ute's Characteristics[23]

Displacement	1,646 tons
Length	205 feet

---

[21] NAVSOURCE Online, Service Ship Photo Archive, http://www.navsource.org/archives/09/39/3907.htm.

[22] Ibid.

[23] Ibid.

Beam	38 ½ feet
Draft	15' 3"
Top Speed	16 knots
Complement	6 Officers 70 enlisted
Armament	One 3"/50 gun mount Two 50 cal machine gun mounts and small arms
Propulsion	Diesel-Electric Four General Motors main engines driving four General Electric generators providing electrical power to four electric drive motors Single Screw 3600 Shaft Horsepower

After climbing the brow to board the Ute, I asked to see the Captain. The quarterdeck watch on duty at the head of the brow asked me who I was. I told the sailor that I was the Ute's new XO. The poor kid's jaw dropped, and he immediately came to attention.

"Yes sir, I'll call him," he said.

He then picked up the ship's intercom phone and called the XO, the officer I was to replace. A moment later, I was shaking hands with LT Mike, the soon to depart XO of the Ute.

As expected, LT Mike was overjoyed to see me, since my reporting meant that he could soon move to his next assignment. LT Mike had an interesting background. He was a Navy Mustang, having come up through the ranks after starting his career as an enlisted sailor, and then moving into the officer ranks. Therefore, he had a wealth of knowledge that certainly helped him succeed as a ship's executive officer.

Mike showed me to a spare stateroom where I could stow my gear. He then took me to meet the Captain. With probably visible trepidation, I entered the CO's cabin and met LT Archie, the ship's captain. Archie and I shook hands and exchanged pleasantries. He asked me about my previous Navy assignments. After I related my MSO experience, I could tell he was not exactly impressed. He was losing a seasoned XO who had been on the Ute for two years, and he was gaining a raw rookie junior officer with limited experience. Additionally, my sea time record on MSOs was pretty meager. The MSOs on which I had served had never been deployed on a cruise. Captain Archie probably felt that he was in big trouble with me as his second in command of the ship.

LT Mike and I left the CO's cabin, and we began the lengthy process of sharing everything I would need to know to take over as XO (yeah right), and the physical signing over to me of classified documents, controlled medicinal drugs, and the XO's .45 caliber pistol. This process took most of the rest of the day and part of the next. Mike's orders allowed him to stay on the ship for the first week I was there, and then depart for his next duty.

In a day or two, the Ute received a work order to tow a gunnery target for another ship on the firing range. As I had done on previous ships, I once again stood at the back of the bridge as the Ute was prepared for sea to watch and absorb the procedures for getting this 205-foot ship (33 feet longer than an MSO) away from the pier and on its way. This procedure was slightly different from the MSOs, as the Ute only had a single screw, versus the twin screw MSOs. Therefore, the method used to distance the ship's stern away from the pier prior to backing the ship away from the pier was not the same as the MSOs. We backed away from the pier, and then waited as a yard tug brought a towable target sled to us. This was the target we would tow for another ship's gunnery practice. We tied off the target to be towed on a short line behind the ship as we cleared Subic Bay harbor. After clearing the harbor, we extended a great deal more towing line to put distance between the target and our ship. Things were going fine, until we cleared buoy one, the outermost harbor buoy. The Ute then commenced rocking and rolling in the sea swells, and the seasickness hit me—big time. I had not been to sea for months, and I was truly sick. I stumbled my way back to my stateroom and lay down. As long as I was lying down, I was fine.

Well, this was a fine spectacle; the new XO crashed out green with seasickness lying in his bunk. I was so embarrassed. But I was also so sick I just wanted to die. If you have ever been seasick you will know what I mean. You truly just want to die quickly to get it over with. I knew that I had lost face with the CO and with the crew, but it could not be helped. Late in the afternoon while we were still at sea, I managed to crawl out of the bunk and make my way to the bridge. If I was in the fresh air and could watch the horizon, I was able to stay vertical. But the damage to my persona had been done, and it would undoubtedly take time for me to earn a bit of respect.

Back in port, in a day or two, LT Mike departed the ship, and I was now on my own as the XO, serving under a seasoned CO who had serious doubts about his new Executive Officer. And I could not blame him; I, too, had doubts about myself.

Captain Archie was also a Navy Mustang. He had been an enlisted quartermaster and rose up through the ranks to transfer to a commissioned officer. He was several inches shorter than I was and had a stocky, powerful body. He gave the appearance of being overweight, but he really was not. Short, stocky, and strong was a better description. During the next few days we got to know each other a bit better, but I am sure his feelings toward me had not changed. He was still very doubtful that I would make it as the Executive Officer. He had a gravelly, low voice. He did not lose his temper often, but when he did, stay out of the way. You did not want to be on the receiving end of a salvo from him. Fortunately, the crew on the Ute was made up of a large core of very experienced men who knew their jobs, and things generally went operationally smooth on the ship. Not only that, but Captain Archie also knew seemingly every job on the ship and was aware immediately when something was amiss and needed attention. He would let me know in no uncertain terms when something on the ship required action. The CO and I soon settled into a routine and got along well, but I always sensed that Archie was watching me to see if I would work out for him in the long run and be a good leader for the ship.

The Ute Wardroom

In the XO's position on the ship, I did not stand duty. The wardroom had four junior officers. Ensign Adam was the Supply Officer, LTJG Rob was the Deck Officer/First Lieutenant, LTJG Pat was the Operations Officer, and Warrant Officer (WO) Cobie was the Chief Engineer. This was the first time I had worked with a WO, and I soon learned some lessons.

Navy Warrant Officers are a class of officers between the enlisted ranks and the commissioned officers. They all come through the enlisted ranks gaining experience along the way. To be a WO, an individual must be well trained and highly skilled in his/her respective enlisted job classification. He or she would then need to apply for the WO program, and acceptance is not automatic. So, most WOs are very knowledgeable in their jobs and proud of the fact that they were picked to become a WO. With WO Cobie, the Chief Engineer, I soon learned how deep this pride runs.

Each morning, I held officer call and muster on the ship. The department heads would meet with me, and I would outline any news and plans for the day. The department heads would then hold quarters and muster with their respective departments. Very soon after reporting aboard the Ute, I was holding morning quarters with the officers and informed them that I would be conducting a physical inspection of their respective departments. I wanted each of them to accompany me as I went through his area of responsibility. This would serve two purposes— it would tell me how they managed their respective departments, and it would help me learn more about the overall operation of the ship and the various departments.

WO Cobie's reaction was, "I don't need the XO to come into my spaces. The engine room is my responsibility, and I don't want you down there."

I was a bit taken aback by his small demonstration of disrespect, but simply told Cobie that we would talk about it more later. I held the inspection in the other three departments and then went looking for Cobie. I found him on the fantail.

Cobie's physical appearance is worth mentioning. Cobie was a tall, well-built guy, with broad shoulders and no extra weight. But his most noticeable feature was his mustache. He had a huge, long handlebar mustache. (Remember those Z-Grams?) He was proud of this mustache and kept it trimmed and waxed so the ends stayed together as they swept up on the side of his face. It certainly was not my cup of tea, but it was within regulation.

I began talking with Cobie and told him I was going to go look in his spaces and engine room.

He puffed his cheeks and was about to voice an objection, but thought better of it, and huffed, "All right, let's go."

So we climbed down the ladders to the engine room, and I looked around. Just like all ships' engine rooms, it was a tremendously noisy, hot, and crowded area. Four huge General Motors engines, each over six feet tall, were spaced across the engine room. The Ute was a diesel, electric powered ship. The diesels turned the generators; the generators provided electricity to the electric motors, which were coupled to the reduction gears, which then turned the giant shaft on which the underwater propeller was attached. The ship had one propeller, but with 3600 shaft horsepower, this small ship was tremendously powerful.

A funny thing happened down there in that engine room. Cobie was now in his element. He loved this mechanical cacophony. He was home. He took me under his wing, and we duck-walked and crawled around the engine room while he pointed out all the equipment and the various electrical power boards, which controlled all aspects of the ship's heart. And he had a grin on his face. He was proud of the shape of the ship's engine room. It was as clean, shiny, and grease free as a hard working navy ship's power plant could be. Being a gear head myself, I asked him a lot of questions about the machinery and how everything worked. It turned out that the thing Cobie feared most was getting an XO who would keep a continual finger in his business as Chief Engineer. I told him that I did not manage that way. I always felt that if an individual did his best job and played according to the rules so that his area of responsibility could stand up to hard work and periodic inspection, then I would leave that individual alone to do his job. But I would jump in with both feet if a subordinate did not do his job satisfactorily. From then on, WO Cobie and I had a good working relationship. I left him alone and stayed out of the engine room unless there was an inspection, and he carried out his responsibilities. I was confident that the Ute's power plant was in good hands.

Two of the junior officers were married, and two were single. They were all great guys, and we spent quite a bit of time together off the ship, as well as while we were working. During the entire time I was on the Ute, there was only one incident with an officer that required disciplinary attention. I will explain that later.

Subic Bay and Olongapo City

Five cannibals were employed by the Navy as translators during one of the island campaigns of World War II. When the CO of the task force welcomed the cannibals he said, "You're all part of our team now. We will compensate you well for your services, and you can eat any of the rations that the sailors are eating. Please do not indulge yourselves by eating a sailor." The cannibals promised. Four weeks later, the CO returned and said, "You're all working hard, and I'm very satisfied with every one of you. However, one of our Chief Petty Officers has disappeared. Do any of you know what happened to him?" The cannibals all shook their heads. After the CO left, the leader of the cannibals turned to the others and said, "Which of you idiots ate the Chief?" A hand raised timidly, to which the leader of the cannibals replied, "You idiot! For four weeks we've been eating Ensigns, Lieutenants, Lieutenant Commanders, Commanders, and even a Captain, and no one even noticed. And then YOU had to go and eat a Chief!"

—Author unknown

After a few days while still in port at Subic Bay, I wanted to leave the ship to do some exploring. One of the chief petty officers happened to see me, and he asked if I would like to go into town, Olongapo, and have a beer with him and the other chiefs. The Ute had four chiefs onboard. They were a quartermaster chief, an electrician's mate chief, an engineman chief, and a boatswain's mate chief. I needed to become better acquainted with these most senior enlisted men on the ship, so I agreed to accompany them.

I had heard a multitude of stories, colorfully describing the infamous Olongapo City, and I thought it was time that I should see this place.

Olongapo was situated directly outside the gates of the Subic Bay Naval base. Most Western Pacific (WESTPAC) sailors experienced Olongapo because of its proximity to the Navy's largest WESTPAC base at Subic Bay. Words truly cannot describe it. This was at the height of the Vietnam war, and the number of military personnel in the Subic Bay area was huge. All branches of the military had bases and other facilities somewhere close to Subic. The Air Force had Clark Air Base approximately twenty miles from Subic. It had its own version of Olongapo, called Angeles City, three miles outside Clark. There was a marine barracks on the Navy base for security, so there were usually plenty of marines on liberty in Olongapo. The Navy base had row after row of ships, and two aircraft carriers rotated on station off Vietnam. Therefore, one carrier was generally in port.

My point here is that thousands of military personnel passed through Subic Bay during the Vietnam era, spending millions of dollars while they were on liberty in Olongapo. This mass of U.S. military personnel spending their money was a huge boost to the Philippine economy. Oh, and the tales that can be told about the area at that time in history!

Two sailors walk past a bar... Well, it **could** *happen!*
—Author unknown

Internet research will reveal that many stories have been written about liberty in Olongapo. The biblical stories of Sodom and Gomorrah should probably be amended to include Olongapo. The city was wide open for almost any vice or colorful pastime that a lonely sailor/soldier was seeking. To go to Olongapo, sailors left the security gate at the base and then crossed a small, filthy river which carried raw sewage and refuse from the city. The stench of the river was overpowering. Hence the sailors simply called the river, "Shit River." As you walked across the bridge into the city, in the water below the bridge young boys were in small dugout boats shouting out that they wanted you to throw them a coin. If a pedestrian threw a coin, the boy would dive out of the canoe and into the fetid, disease-laden water to retrieve the coin. I always shuddered as I watched these boys disappear into that sewer water. It seemed to me that there was no way for those kids to remain disease free after swimming in that sewage.

The main street of Olongapo, which began just across the river, was jam-packed with bars and clubs catering to the visitors. The loud, electronically amplified music blared from every open bar's doorway and could be heard even before a sailor reached the city. Continuing on, you then entered the city and came to the money changers, who would exchange your American dollars for Philippine pesos. No one ever knew if the money changers gave the correct, fair amount of pesos for an American dollar.

After that, you headed down the dirt main street looking for a bar to get a beer and maybe some food. Every business establishment could be identified by huge, gaudy lights and signs, beckoning the passersby to come into that place of business. Some even had an employee sitting on a stool on the sidewalk outside the business with an electric bull horn, or microphone urging the pedestrian to come inside where it was cool, and the beer was ice cold.

The next thing to hit a person was the sheer noise of the little city. The traffic was intense on the dirt streets, and the sound of honking horns was almost constant.

The main mode of passenger transport was the "Jeepney." Jeepneys were World War II Jeeps that had been greatly modified to include a rear portion that would hold eight or more passengers. Each Jeepney owner tried to outdo his competition by having the most wild, colorful paint job imaginable. Lights, mirrors, and every conceivable piece of chrome hung on the Jeepneys. They were the most gaudy motorized vehicle that I had ever seen. The drivers were all fearless and drove as fast as they possibly could, narrowly missing each other in the crowded traffic conditions. Each Jeepney had a radio that was amped up, also to outdo its competition, in order to be the wildest, loudest guy on the street. Jeepneys were super cheap to ride from one end of town to another, and we would jump on one and throw a few pesos to the driver when we departed. I always thought it would be fun to have one of those crazy vehicles. All this was part of the sensory overload one saw in Olongapo.

In every bar, there were a large number of young girls acting as hostesses. They were there to sell you drinks. And some of them also took on other duties as prostitutes. The very aggressive prostitutes wandered through all the bars. There were also pick-pockets, and other shady types who kept on the lookout for military guys who had too much to drink. The unsuspecting military guy might then be coerced into following a shady character to a back alley and being relieved of his watch, rings, and money by other cronies. Fights were not uncommon, but were quickly subdued by the ever present shore patrol. Needless to say, lonely, thirsty, hungry sailors and marines loved this place. I could go into a great deal of detail about this nasty WESTPAC icon, but it could require another whole book. Without a doubt, a Sodom or Gomorrah resident would have felt right at home.

So the Ute's chiefs had decided to introduce me to Olongapo. Naturally, I was agog at this strange world. It was sensory overload for a 23-

year-old from Iowa. But I had previously heard enough about Olongapo to have a good idea what the chiefs were up to, and I played along with them. After several beers, one of the bar prostitutes came to our table and was "assigned" to me by the chiefs. The chiefs were determined to properly "initiate" their new XO. I played along, and as the night went on, more alcohol was consumed. Finally, it was time to return to the ship before curfew, unless you rented a hotel room and stayed overnight in town, which was permissible.

As we walked toward the base, the prostitute seemed to be tagging along with us. Then, I found myself surrounded by the four chiefs who eased me into one of the seedy hotel lobbies with the prostitute in tow. I still played along, and after all arrangements were made, the chiefs headed out of the hotel and back to the Navy base gate. I watched them leave and waited in the lobby. After a bit, I gave the prostitute some pesos for her trouble, and I left the hotel. It was close to curfew, which meant that the base gate would close, locking out anyone caught in the city after curfew. I managed to arrive at the gate with only a couple of minutes to spare.

When I reached the ship, all was quiet, and I slipped into my stateroom and crashed. The next morning, the joke on the ship was that the XO had been "initiated" in Olongapo the night before. I did not say a word and let them have their little joke. But inwardly, I had the last laugh. In all my time overseas, I always kept my sweet wife in my thoughts and prayers, never doing anything to hurt her or degrade myself. And it has stayed that way through 42-plus years of marriage.

Another of the tricks of the street people in Olongapo was the wrist watch theft. To accomplish this, a character would sidle up to a sailor, grasp the face of the sailor's wrist watch, and make a sharp twist of the watch. This would either break the watch band or the pins holding the watch to the watch band. The thief would then take off running at top speed. The poor inebriated sailor did not even know it had happened, until it was too late to chase the perpetrator.

While Olongapo was really a despicable sort of place, after a while one tended to get used to the strange seediness, and I usually went into the city two or three times a week while we were in port. The national beer of the Philippines is San Miguel. The beer was good, and it was cheap. I found a couple of bars that were quieter, where I could have ice cold San Miguel beers, watch the strange goings on in the place, and talk to other guys before heading back to the ship. I remember sitting in one of these joints talking to the bartender and looking up at a huge sign behind the bar. In big numbers, it stated that a San Miguel beer was sixteen pesos. The conversion rate at the time meant that the ice cold bottle of beer I was drinking cost the equivalent of an American quarter. Now that's a deal! I also would go into some of the gambling places and blow a few bucks on the craps table, have a cold beer, and generally just relax and have some fun. But at the end of my outing, I was always found walking back to the ship.

I usually knew where most of the Ute sailors hung out, and I would periodically go into those bars just to make sure my boys were doing all right and staying out of trouble. They were a good bunch of guys, though, and they socialized together most of the time. Several guys on the ship played musical instruments, guitars and drums, and I had heard them practicing on the ship. One afternoon, a group of them were excited because their little band had been booked to play in one of their favorite Olongapo bar hang-outs. After they had played for a couple of nights, they asked me to come to the bar to hear them. So LTJG Pat and I went to the bar that night to listen to them. They were wailing away on the latest American rock songs and just having a great time. When they finally took a break, they came over to our table and sat down with Pat and me.

At some point in the conversation, while under the influence of San Miguel, I asked if I could sing with them. Oh, horrors. They did not know what to answer. Since I was the XO, they did not want to offend me, but they also did not want to embarrass their fledgling band by having some lunatic sing an off-key rendering of rock and roll. After I told them what I would sing, they finally agreed to let me have the microphone. Nobody on the ship knew I could sing. After all, they thought I was too mean to be a singer. But all went well. I sang a couple songs; the band was totally shocked, and from then on, when I went to see the band, they always asked me to sing.

Their little band was unique in Olongapo. Many of the bars had rock bands, but they were all comprised of Filipinos, and the band members' English was limited. As a result, you might recognize the tune, but there was no way you could understand the lyrics. Although sometimes comical, we never enjoyed that music very much. When word got out that there was an American rock band playing in a local bar, patronage at that bar increased considerably. My guys were happy, and the bar owner was even happier.

The sailors on the ship adopted a popular hit song to be the ship's theme song. It was the John Denver song called "Country Roads." For us, it was a bit melancholy and reminded all of us that we would much rather be at home instead of in a foreign land. When the ship's band was playing in the bar, or at any other time, "Country Roads" would always be part of their repertoire. And every time we heard it, the guys would become quiet and think of their loved ones back home. Even grown men, who had been away from home many times, could be homesick.

Along the sidewalk as we returned to the base, we would pass vendors selling chewing gum, cigarettes, or other knick-knacks. But there were also barbecue vendors. Ensign Adam introduced me to this treat one night as we headed back to the ship.

He said, "XO, have you ever had monkey meat?"

Of course I told him I had not. We stopped at a little Hibachi grill where a withered old woman was tending her grill which contained bamboo sticks with some sort of meat impaled on them. We bought a few and kept heading toward the ship as we ate. From then on I was hooked. The meat was probably poor cuts of pork or chicken, but we always called it monkey meat. In addition, we always laughed that the only dogs we saw in Olongapo were usually being chased by a guy with a cleaver. What we were eating really was a mystery, but it sure was a great snack at the end of the evening.

Time Bomb

One night on my way back to the base, I passed a guy selling watches. Wrist watches were a fetish thing with the Filipino guys. They wanted to wear the biggest, fanciest, shiniest watch to outdo their buddies. Many of the U.S. sailors were of the same mindset. So there were always several vendors selling watches on the street. You would walk by, and they would hold up their arms, showing ten or more watches strapped to their arms.

They would say, "Hey sailor, want to buy watch?"

Usually, I would ignore them and keep walking, but a couple of days prior to this, I had purchased a new Seiko watch at the Navy Exchange, and I now had an extra one. I had been wearing an old Timex, because I did not want to have a good watch stolen from me on the street in Olongapo. I did not really need the old Timex anymore, but I was still wearing it.

So, as I passed one of these vendors who asked me if I wanted to buy a watch, I turned to him and said, "Hey, do *you* wanna buy a watch?"

He asked to look at it, and I showed him my Timex. His immediate reaction was amusing.

He said, "Oh no, a Time Bomb (Timex). Don't want."

I laughed and said, "No, it is a great watch. How much will you give me for the watch?"

We haggled back and forth for a while. Another vendor, who was selling cheap oil paintings nearby, had been watching our dialogue with rapt attention, so I decided to include him in the negotiations. This went on for a while, and we were all having fun. When the yakking was done, the watch vendor had bought my old Timex for ten dollars and threw in an oil painting from the other vendor. I chuckled all the way back to the ship. Jan and I kept that painting of a Philippine country scene hanging in our house for quite some time, until she finally insisted that it find another home.

The Weather

The weather at Subic Bay was something that I never grew to appreciate. Most of my life had been spent in the upper Midwest of the United States, and the Philippine weather was immensely stifling to me. Temperatures in the upper nineties were common, with an accompanying humidity also in the nineties. A couple of minutes outside any air conditioning left a person soaked in perspiration with their clothing clinging to them.

The strangest part of the weather was the "rainy season." Frankly, I thought the entire calendar year was the rainy season. During the rainy season especially, there was never a light, gentle shower. The rain came down like I had never seen before. You have undoubtedly heard the term; "rain coming down in sheets." But try to imagine rain so thick and fast that you cannot see even fifty feet in front of your line of sight. There were literal sheets of falling water from one to three times per day during the rainy season. I recall one day in port while standing on the bridge of the Ute during a rainstorm. The water was coming down so densely that I could not see the building adjacent to the pier where the ship was tied. I stood there shaking my head in wonder—while my polyester khaki uniform remained stuck to my body. The Philippines is a beautiful country with many exotic varieties of plants and wildlife, but the weather is tough for non-natives.

Because of the tropical temperatures and humidity, weather at sea was sometimes quite dramatic. In most cases while the ship was in transit, we were able to receive Navy weather reports for the regions where we operated. Because of this, we sometimes changed the ship's course to avoid typhoons or severe and dangerous weather. In spite of precautions, we were in numerous storms that we thought would tear the ship apart. But the little Ute was tougher than she looked, and she weathered the storms to keep us all safe.

Waterspouts were an interesting phenomena that we often saw in our ocean travels. These huge, tall, undulating columns of spinning water are cyclonic storms, similar to tornados, but they occur over open water. Having grown up in landlocked Iowa, waterspouts were fascinating to me. I learned that waterspouts are not nearly as powerful as tornados, but are still a wondrous show of the beauty and power of nature.

Beer Baseball and Other Fun

As you have gathered, it was not all work and no play while we were in port. In addition to our other, maybe not so healthy activities, the Ute had a baseball team. When I came aboard the ship and attended my first ship's baseball game, I was shocked by how good they were! The team played fast pitch softball and would play challenge games against other ships or military units in the Subic area. Captain Archie was the team's pitcher, and he was terrific. Many of our wins were simply because the other teams' batters could not hit Archie's fast ball pitches. I had played church league softball in my college days, and I wanted to play on the team. I told the team captain, one of the enlisted guys, that I would like to play first base. I usually played first, because I did not have a fielder's arm, but I could catch anything thrown my way and could hit well. Uh, oh. Another of those instances where the crew team members did not know my capabilities, but they almost had to give the ship's XO a spot on the team. So, in next game, I took the field and proved to them that I deserved the position I had requested. I hit well, scored a run or two, and snagged all balls thrown to me. From then on, I was a regular on the team.

I used the term beer baseball, because each team arrived at the playing field with its own large galvanized trash can filled with beer, soda, and ice. During the game, this ice cold refreshment was consumed by the teams to stay cool. Remember, temperatures and humidity necessitated staying hydrated. So we did. By the end of the game, the barrels were usually empty and both teams were hot, sweaty, and happy. Preparations for beer baseball games had been made before the Ute left for deployment from Hawaii. We used Morale Welfare and Recreation funds to stock up on beer at the Navy Exchange and loaded it into a locked storeroom on the ship. The beers of choice were the Hawaiian beer called Primo, and the West Coast Olympia beer, nicknamed Oley, primarily because these two brands were the least expensive and were popular with everyone.

The Ute had only seventy-five guys from which to choose a baseball team with back-ups. But our team played against other ships having from several hundred to a couple of thousand sailors from which to draw baseball talent. Not only did we play other service ships in our squadron, but we even played against the mighty Kitty Hawk aircraft carrier. We beat them all! No, we did not win every single game, but our average was probably in excess of 80% wins. Once in a while we would play against a larger ship's team that would swagger onto the field in their custom-made uniforms and great, expensive ball gear. They would laugh and look down their noses at our scruffy looking team and know that there would be no contest. We played in tee shirts and shorts or jeans. Our entire uniform consisted of matching ball caps. We always felt good when we beat a cocky team from a big ship, and we usually did.

I recall one afternoon's baseball game. It was so hot and steamy that you just wanted to relax somewhere in the shade and not move. But we were playing baseball. We were playing one of the large oiler ships, a periodic rival. The game progressed, and the score was close. The other team was at bat, and I was playing first base. The opposing team player hit the ball, and it was fielded. I stood out of the base path, with just the edge of my left foot touching the right side of the bag and waited for the throw. As the ball hit my glove for the out, the big meat-head guy running the base line for first, jumped and landed on my ankle, which was next to the first base bag. His action is what is known as a dirty play. He had intentionally landed on the infield side of the bag to hit my ankle, when he had the whole bag to step on. I screamed in pain and hopped off the field. I thought my ankle was broken. I was enraged, and I watched this buzzard sauntering his way to his side's bench.

At that moment, I wound up and threw the ball at him as hard as I could. The ball whizzed by his ear, and he spun around and started to charge me. I was ready for him, but then I noticed that the rest of his teammates were streaming off their bench and also heading for me. Uh, oh, and I couldn't even walk, let alone run. But suddenly, running up beside me was the rest of the Ute team. The odds just got better, and we were ready for the melee. I yelled at the guy that had stomped me that he was a chicken shit, and a dirty player, and that he was out by a mile. He had no cause to do what he did.

Things began to look like it would come to blows. But just then, Captain Archie got between the two teams, and a member of the other team did the same. These cooler heads prevailed, of course, and we declared the game over with the Ute the winner since we were ahead. Then both the beer barrels were dragged out onto the center of the field, and more beer drinking ensued. The gorilla who had stomped me finally came over as we continued to imbibe and apologized for his cheap shot.

I learned two things from that game. First, never intentionally throw a baseball at an opposing team member when you are playing a position right next to their dugout, and second, the Ute guys thought enough of their XO that they came to my aid, even though I had done something stupid on my own. I love a happy ending, don't you?

I have no idea how many sweaty baseball games I played while attached to the Ute, but they were always spirited fun.

Another of our favorite off-duty pastimes was snorkeling and scuba diving. Because it was a salvage ship, the Ute had two qualified Navy-trained divers onboard; one officer and one enlisted crew member. LTJG Pat was the diving officer for the ship. He, the enlisted diver, and I, along with a few other members of the crew, would often go to Grande Island to dive. The waters around the Philippines were beautifully clear and teaming with tropical fish and marine life of every color and description. This was my first exposure to ocean diving, and I became hooked on it. No pun intended—or maybe it was intentional. Anyway, a whole new, wondrous, and beautiful world opened up to me.

From the Subic Navy Base, the recreational services folks ran a shuttle boat that took passengers to the little island called Grande Island, a few miles from the base. Grande Island also had a little concession area which sold food and drinks, and where rental cabins were available for overnight stays. Our little group would hop on the boat to go diving for the day. The ship's divers could scuba dive, because they were qualified divers, but the rest of us could only snorkel, as we had not yet qualified for scuba gear.

Even the snorkeling was truly amazing. The reefs varied in water depth, so that a snorkeler viewed undersea life much the same as the scuba divers, although they went deeper. I was fascinated as I explored the new and amazing sights along the reefs.

Among the sea life were usually some black tip sharks. The two scuba divers did not fear them, but I kept them at a healthy distance. Black tip sharks are usually wary of humans, but are also known to attack humans if they think there is other food in the area. The divers teased me after they surfaced and facetiously thanked me for being the surface bait while they were diving. I did not think that was all that funny. In addition to the black tips, periodically we would see hammerhead sharks. Hammerheads are a bit less predictable, and even the scuba divers would leave the water for a while when the hammerheads showed up.

We would dive and snorkel most of the day, pausing to lay on the beach in the shade and eat lunch. By the end of the day, we were wiped out and hopped the boat back to the base. We spent many enjoyable days diving in the Philippines. I enjoyed it so much that after the first cruise, when the ship returned to Pearl Harbor, I enrolled in a scuba class and became certified so that I could scuba dive on the next cruise.

Another activity was a fantail skeet shoot. Members of the crew were allowed to bring their own personal shot guns onto the ship prior to the ship's deployment. These guns were locked up in the ship's small arms armory. The ship would also buy a supply of clay pigeons and shot gun ammunition. When the Ute was at sea, skeet shoot contests were held on the fantail. While the skeet shoot was held, the cooks would bring out barbeque grills and cook steaks for a good steak picnic for all hands at the conclusion of the skeet shoot. Of course, this activity only worked well when the seas would cooperate with a nice smooth day.

Many of the guys liked to try their hand at fishing and would trail a baited line off the fantail of the ship while we were underway. I don't remember what the guys used for bait, but it seemed like we caught a disproportionate number of small sharks. These were always thrown back. If someone caught a larger shark, the crew would gather around it and ooh and aah before it was returned to the sea. One of our Filipino stewards loved to fish, and he could be found on the fantail fishing quite often. When he caught edible fish, he would clean, and cook them for the other stewards and the wardroom. It was always a treat to have a fresh fish dinner. Some of the crew members would do the same, and if enough fish were caught, the cooks would prepare the fish for the crew's meal.

Almost every night in port, and also at sea if the sea and weather permitted, movies were shown on the fantail of the Ute. We rigged up a white screen from the crane boom, and everyone would find a place to sit on the deck, or on a piece of machinery to watch the movie. Trading movies with other ships in port was a big deal, and we were always trying to find movies we had not seen before. The movies were usually quite new, often first-run movies that would be showing in theaters back in the states. Action movies were always a big hit with the young guys. Chick flicks and/or love stories were usually booed so loudly that the projectionist had to shut down the machine until a male-appropriate replacement movie could be found. Occasionally, one of the cooks would find some popcorn and pop a huge batch for the moviegoers. The sailors would turn their white hats inside-out and use them as popcorn bowls. Just like home, right?

Then there was poker. A few of the crew members liked to play cards or shoot dice. The Navy did not condone this behavior, but it was hard to stop. The first time I saw the guys rolling dice in their quarters, I watched for a minute and walked away. I knew it was a losing battle to try to snuff out this pastime, but I let the department heads and leading petty officers know that the first time I heard of any junior sailor getting fleeced by some shark, I would lower the boom. In later observations, it seemed that the stakes were pretty low in their games. They usually played nickel/dime/quarter type games, and I never heard of anyone getting financially hurt, so I let the games continue, with monitoring. In addition, in a tight-knit group like the Ute sailors, they tended to get along very well. Among the sixty or seventy guys on the Ute, there were no more than four or five troublemaker types whom no one wanted to befriend. Those four or five were the real foul balls, slackers, or druggies, and no one wanted them around. The crew genuinely cared about their buddies and would not allow one of their friends to get hurt physically or financially if they could help it. Therefore, I never saw any high stakes poker games. It was all for fun and camaraderie.

Subic Bay base had two officers' clubs, enlisted clubs, and a chiefs' club on the base, so there were alternatives to going into Olongapo. Our wardroom occasionally went to the larger officers' club for a good meal. The other officers' club was called The Chuck Wagon, and it was located in an old World War II vintage Quonset style building. The Chuckwagon served mostly sandwiches and light fare. The draw there was their slot machines. Captain Archie and I would often go to the Chuckwagon for a burger and a beer and to play the nickel slot machines for a couple hours in the evening. I think the machines must have been rigged, because no one ever seemed to win anything, but no one ever lost very much either. I think my largest loss was two dollars in one evening.

For some very high spirited fun, there was also another Officers' Club. Adjacent to Subic Bay was Naval Air Station Cubi Point. There you would find the notorious Cubi Point Officers' Club. This was a rip-roaring place where all the pilots hung out when they were not flying. The club's walls were covered with the plaques of every air squadron that had operated in WESTPAC. The plaques listed all of the names of the fliers in that squadron with their deployment dates. In addition, the club had the famous tail hook slide. The off-duty pilots would launch themselves, or be launched by other guys, down a long, horizontal slide. Near the end of the slide, the pilot would try to catch himself with his feet (his tail hook) to prevent falling off the end of the slide. Depending upon how much beer had been consumed, the pilot might keep himself from falling off the end of the slide, or if not, he would be doused with pitchers of beer by his fellow pilots, and the resultant laughter would shake the house. We ship drivers who might be visiting the club, thought this was about the most silly, hilarious fun we had ever seen. We loved going there. On weekends, the place was rocking!

I recently had an opportunity to visit the Naval Aviation Museum in Pensacola, Florida. Inside the museum, there is a café that was built to replicate the Cubi Officers' Club, and it reminded me of my visits to the real club, many years ago. The walls of this new café/bar are also covered with the squadron plaques that were brought over from the old Cubi Club for just this purpose. Pretty neat! Unfortunately, there are so many plaques that space limitations have necessitated the oldest ones, including those of the Vietnam era, being stored away and no longer on display.

The enlisted guys preferred going into town. But sailors' pay did not stretch very far, and as payday approached, they were usually low on funds. To accommodate this common problem, the enlisted club on the base set aside the night before payday as "Poor Boy Night." On that night, the enlisted club had special ten-cent drinks, and correspondingly cheap food. The guys were then able to have a good time on just a couple bucks. Sometimes, too much of a good time.

Monkey Golf

Another popular diversion for off-duty time was golf. Close by the base, a really nice golf course had literally been carved out of the jungle. The Navy golf course had fairways and greens that were bordered on all sides by dense jungle and hills, like those found over much of the Philippines. I played golf on this course several times, and certain things stand out in my memory. First, the caddies at the course were Filipino guys who lugged our clubs all around the eighteen holes for just a couple dollars. Even though I did not carry my clubs while walking the course (there were no carts), I would be drenched in sweat from the heat and humidity. The caddies did not complain as they carried our clubs while walking eighteen holes in their flip flop sandals. They were tough guys, and we made a point to tip them well for their efforts.

I remember one particular hole, which was a par four hole. From the tee box, you hit the ball out and up to the top of a high, round hill. The green was on the top of the hill. It was far enough away that your first shot took you only as far as the base of the hill. The second shot would need to be darn near straight up to reach the top of the hill. I have no idea how many strokes it usually took for me to reach the top of the hill, because each time I would take a shot, the ball simply rolled back off the hill to end up at my feet again. It was very frustrating, of course. Assuming that a golfer finally got the ball up on top of the hill, and it stayed there, it became even more interesting. Remember, that hill is almost straight up, so, at the base of the hill, there was a motorized rope and pulley system. The motor pulled a large diameter rope over pulleys to the top of the hill. Because the hill was so steep, each golfer grabbed onto the rope with both hands and let the rope pull him to the top of the hill, while walking/climbing up the hill. It was similar to a ski lift that you hung onto and walked. I had never seen a golf hole with this type of contraption and have not seen one since. It was certainly unique.

I titled this section Monkey Golf for a reason. The jungle adjacent to the golf course was full of native wildlife, including monkeys. The monkeys were thick in that jungle and had an annoying habit. They loved to run out of the jungle and onto the fairways of the golf course, grab a golf ball, and scurry back into the jungle with the ball. Yes, it was comical, but hey, golf balls cost money. No penalty strokes were assigned, and we would just replace the ball when we walked up to where the ball had been lying. I never saw anyone try to get a ball back from the little primates. After all, we were intruding on their territory, and we never knew what else might be lurking in that jungle if we tried to chase one of the little thieves.

Living Conditions on the Ute

I am inserting another, rather long joke here, which circulated in Navy circles for many years, by an unknown author. It is meant to provide you with a humorous look at living conditions onboard old Navy ships. Unfortunately, it rings true, with many tongue-in-cheek comparisons with the Ute's living conditions.

How to Simulate Life Aboard a Navy Ship [Author unknown]
- *Buy a garbage dumpster, paint it gray, and live in it for six months*
- *Run all piping and wiring on the inside walls of your house*
- *Pump 10 inches of dirty, nasty water into your basement, pump it out occasionally and then pump in a new batch*
- *On Mondays, Wednesdays, and Fridays, turn your water temperature up to 200 degrees, and turn it to 10 degrees on Tuesday and Thursday. On Saturday and Sunday, tell your family they used too much water during the week, so there can be no shower those days*
- *Raise your bed to within six inches of the ceiling*
- *Eat the raunchiest Mexican food you can find for three days, then lock yourself out of the bathroom for twelve hours, and hang a sign on the door that reads, "Secured, repairs needed."*
- *Have your mother-in-law write down everything the family is going to do the next day and then have her stand in the back yard at 6 a.m. and read it to the family*
- *Submit a written form to your father-in-law, asking if it is OK to leave the house before three p.m.*
- *Shower with 100 of your not so closest friends*

- *Walk around your car for 4 hours and check the tire pressure every 15 minutes*
- *Sit in your car and let it run for 4 hours before going anywhere, just to ensure that your engine is properly "lit off"*
- *Repaint your entire house once a month*
- *Use fifteen scoops of budget coffee grounds per pot, and allow each pot to sit for four hours before drinking any of it*
- *Have your 5 year old give you a haircut with pinking shears*
- *Spend five years working at McDonalds, and NOT get promoted*
- *When your children are in bed, run into their room with a megaphone, and shout at the top of your lungs that your home is being attacked, and order them to battle stations—General Quarters, General Quarters!*
- *For ambience, leave the lawn mower running in your living room 24 hours a day.*
- *When there is a thunderstorm in your area, find a wobbly rocking chair and rock as hard as you can until you become nauseated. Be sure to have some pink Dramamine pills and stale crackers in your pocket.*
- *Raise the thresholds and lower the top sills of all the doors in your house so that you either trip or bang your head every time you go through one of them.*
- *When baking a cake, prop up one side of the pan while it is in the oven. Spread icing on real thick to level it off.*
- *In the middle of January, place a podium at the end of your driveway, and have a family member stand watch at the podium, rotating family members every four hours.*
- *Post a menu on the refrigerator door informing your family that you are having steak for dinner. Then make them stand in line for at least an hour, and when they finally get to the kitchen, tell them you are out of steak, but you have chipped beef or hot dogs.*
- *Have your next door neighbor come over each day at 5 a.m. and blow a whistle so loud that it could wake the dead, and shout, "Reveille, reveille, all hands heave to and trice up."*

Ok, ok, you get the idea. Living on a little steel ship is not necessarily fun or luxurious. My little XO's cabin was far smaller than today's walk-in closets. It had a bunk, one metal closet, a small sink, and a desk and chair. I shared the single head and shower one deck below with the four junior officers. The junior officers had rooms with two bunks, a closet and a desk. The CO's cabin was about twice the size of my cabin with room for a fold-out couch/bed, and he also had his own head and shower.

But it was the enlisted crew members who really suffered. The crew's berthing area was directly below the steel, fantail deck. The fantail deck caught full sun all day long. As a result, the crew's berthing area was stiflingly hot, day or night. The ship had a watertight hatch that measured about three feet by three feet in size, located on the deck of the fantail, directly above the crew's berthing area. To maintain the ship's watertight integrity, the hatch was supposed to remain closed and sealed when the ship was underway. But if the air conditioning was not working, the berthing compartment was so hot that we allowed the hatch to remain open, even while underway, so that some air could enter the compartment below. Many of the guys would remove their mattresses from their bunks and drag them up on deck on the fantail, sleeping there to get some fresh air and be a bit cooler. In the morning they would drag the mattresses back down the hatch and onto their bunks.

The sixty to seventy enlisted guys shared a head with three showers, three toilets, and four sinks. As you can imagine, the enlisted head was a busy place. While all of the berthing areas were air conditioned, much of the time, the ship's air conditioning did not work. The only location that was vital to keep cool was the ship's radio room. That air conditioning unit was a priority, while berthing areas took second place. The habitual problem was that on a 30-year-old ship, parts were always breaking, and spare parts for the ship's machinery and air conditioning units often had to be ordered from the U.S. It could take weeks for parts to reach us as we sailed around the Western Pacific, if the parts were even available.

It was just coincidental that my little state room was next to the radio shack and across the passageway from the CO's cabin. The air conditioning unit for those three areas was physically located in my state room. The unit was an old floor-to-ceiling monster about four feet wide and three feet deep, thereby making my cabin even cozier. And since the unit was not working at least one-fourth of the time, there were often sailors in my cabin trying to make repairs to that air conditioning unit. It was not unusual to step over crew members to enter my cabin. I recall trying to go to sleep one night as four guys with wrenches were sprawled around the room, next to my head, banging on pipes as they carried out their repair work. That memory reminds me of an old black and white Marx brothers' comedy movie ("Night at the Opera") in which fifteen people, including plumbers and luggage, were trying to enter one very small shipboard cabin. What a comedy. When our environment was one hundred degrees Fahrenheit, with a matching humidity, we all prayed our thanks to the inventor of air conditioning, and it was a real blessing when our crew could keep those machines working.

The manual labor undertaken by the sailors on the Ute was extremely dirty, sweaty work. The guys would end up filthy after working to rig a tow for the ship. Being able to shower and have clean clothes was a wonderful, but unfortunately rare, occasion. The ship's laundry consisted of one clothes washer and one dryer, similar in size to those found in the average home. You can quickly visualize the scene; seventy-five hot, sweaty, dirty, stinky men trying to have clean clothes once in a while at sea. It was almost an impossibility. If the washer and dryer were not broken, you might have clean clothes once a week, that is, if the ship had enough water.

The Ute's biggest problem at sea was having sufficient fresh water. The ship's evaporator system worked to produce fresh water by heating sea water and capturing the condensation, thereby purifying and removing the salt from the sea water. The old evaporator was probably the same age as the ship and was unable to keep up with the demand for cooking, drinking, and bathing water. As a result, if the ship was at sea for four or more days, which happened often, the showers in the heads would have to be turned off—no showers. And the laundry would also be closed to conserve water. Imagine the lovely scent of that ship with seventy-five unwashed savages in close proximity to each other. I have to tell you, a person can get used to it, because we all smelled equally as bad.

Food on the ship was generally quite good and nutritious, although rather bland. Navy cooks were required to strictly follow the established Navy cooking recipes. I think those recipes may have originated in the First World War. None of the food had any flair, and it made you yearn for something in the way of a good meal. To make matters worse, one of the senior cooks was constantly seasick. His seasickness would leave the galley cooks shorthanded, creating problems in getting meals prepared on time and meals that were tasty.

Unlike large ships, where the officers buy their own food and have it prepared by cooks for the wardroom, on a small ship like the Ute, the officers ate the same food as the crew and still had to pay for it. The wardroom stewards would simply fill serving dishes from the galley and bring them into the wardroom for the officers. In one respect this was good, because the sailors could never say that the officers ate better than the crew. One exception was that our stewards were Filipino men, and they missed their home country's cooking. So once in a while, they would gather the necessary ingredients and prepare a batch of Filipino fare, making sure they made enough for the wardroom. Those meals were a real treat from the standard Navy chow.

Eating while underway was a real challenge. Imagine sitting down at your family dining table to eat a meal while the floor of your dining room is rolling back and forth like a Disneyland "E ticket" ride, and the table keeps sloping up and down with each side rising and falling as much as a foot with each roll cycle of the dining room. Nothing will remain on the table. It will end up in each diner's lap or on the deck. And your stomach is taking the same trip as the table. Sound like fun? Such was eating underway on the Ute. To minimize movement of dishes and utensils, we had a wooden device that fit on top of the wardroom dining table. It was called a "fiddle" or "fiddle rail," and it fit over the edge of the table, resulting in a rail around the perimeter of the table about three inches high. This batten, or rim, also had partitions running across the table lengthwise and crosswise. These partitions kept the plates, utensils, and service items from sliding off the table, but it did not prevent items from spilling onto the table. Although it kept most items from shooting completely off of the table, there were times when even this three inch batten could not keep dishes from flying off and crashing to the deck, or onto an unlucky eater's lap. The enlisted crew ate at longer tables, and unfortunately they did not have fiddle rails on their tables. Because the officers' wardroom was situated very close to the mess decks, we could often hear the crashing of metal food trays, or dishes, flying off the tables onto the steel dining room decks. There were many days at sea when it was simply too rough and dangerous to cook on the ship. On those days, the cooks would make cold cut sandwiches for everyone instead of hot meals.

If it moves, salute it. If it doesn't move, paint it!
—Author unknown

Although that old Navy saw may be a bit humorous, there is also considerable truth in it. Steel Navy ships need constant maintenance and painting to keep them from rusting away. One section of the deck gang chipped and painted virtually every day on the Ute, whether we were in port or underway. In addition to hand scrapers, to facilitate removing the old flaky paint and rust, the gang also used needle guns. Whether air driven or electric, these devices resembled large handguns. But the barrel was comprised of a cluster of sharp rods protruding from the front. When the gun was switched on, these rods would alternately shoot back and forth in the end of the gun. The gun barrel would be held against the steel to be painted, and the vibrating rods would chip off the old paint and rust to ready the surface for the new paint. The drawback was that these needle guns were extremely loud. They were so loud, that when one was operating, the steel of the ship acted as a sound conductor, and the noise could be heard throughout the ship. Some of the crew knew how much I disliked the noise of those machines, and sometimes I got the impression that the crew would find out where I was working on the ship that day and set up their needle gun chorus near my work station, just to needle me. (Groan.)

After an area was prepared for painting, at least one coat of primer, and sometimes two coats of primer were used, followed by the ubiquitous Navy gray. But operating in the warm tropics with a heavy travel schedule often meant that cosmetics took a back seat to mission, and the Ute always had visible rust areas calling out for maintenance. Periods of in port time gave the crew opportunities to catch up on maintenance, but often, these in port times were sporadic. Hence, Ute always looked like a working ship; a bit scruffy around the edges, but with a stout heart.

The Mean Old XO

As I mentioned before, by virtue of the mission of the ship, the work was dirty and dangerous on board the Ute. As such, most of the time the appearance of the men in their work uniforms would not win any Navy good grooming awards. These were manual labor, sweating, working guys, on a working Navy ship—the blue collar work force for the Navy. But I was determined that when the men were not working, they would keep themselves and their living areas neat and clean. In my daily rounds and inspection of the ship, I became more and more disgusted with the way the crew lived in their berthing area. The enlisted quarters looked like home to fifty undisciplined teenage boys. Clothing was flung all over the deck, bunks were not made up, the deck was always dirty, and the place reeked. I took on a mission.

One day, I told all of the chiefs and the first class petty officers to meet me in the enlisted berthing area after morning quarters. They all appeared, and I stood just inside the water tight door to the compartment. I did not say a word to begin with. I wanted them to simply take in the scene and atmosphere. A couple of these senior petty officers got it. From the look on their faces, I could tell they understood why I had brought them there. I then told them that as the senior sailors on the ship, they were responsible for the living conditions, the sanitation, the military bearing, the safety, and training of their men. I then told them that they had failed in this area and asked them how long it had been since they had inspected this pig sty. We then went up to the enlisted head. A similar mess greeted us there. The showers, toilets, sinks, and deck all needed scrubbing with steel wool and disinfectant. What a mess! From that point on, I told them that a senior petty officer would be assigned on a daily basis to be responsible for the cleanliness, neatness, and seaworthiness of the enlisted quarters. They were to work out a rotation schedule among themselves for that responsibility. I would not allow the crew to live like animals. In short, the senior petty officers hated it, and the crew hated it! I am sure they thought the XO was an unreasonable meanie. Apparently, the crew had been allowed to live like pigs in their quarters for a long time.

Next, I brought the junior officers down to the enlisted berthing area and had them view the situation. I gave them the same lecture. They were responsible for the training, cleanliness, and safety of their assigned men. But the real kicker came when I told them that all hands would be confined to the ship and there would be no liberty if the enlisted quarters did not meet my expectations at morning inspections. I told them I did not care how this task was carried out, but the next day, the enlisted quarters had better pass a close inspection. I then left them to work out the problem. You would have thought that a major catastrophe had occurred. On a small ship, the CO soon knows everything that is going on, and he soon had an earful of what I was doing. But Captain Archie was no fool. He knew that the enlisted quarters were a mess, and he backed me up one hundred percent.

Over the course of the next three days, the appearance and cleanliness of the enlisted quarters improved. Each morning, a work party was assigned to clean these areas. The crew began to take pride in the way their quarters looked, and they grew accustomed to keeping the area clean. I continued to inspect every day and before liberty call. I was pleased to see that the ship began to look a whole lot better.

Next, I began working on the crew's military appearance. Many of the men had taken the Z-Gram appearance standards way too far. Haircuts and facial hair on the majority of the men did not conform to Navy standards. So again, the issue was addressed with the officers and senior petty officers. Once again, the XO was being a bad guy, and side comments and complaints reached the CO. And once again, the CO backed me up. The men got their much-needed haircuts and trims, and now the crew was also looking better. These issues needed continual monitoring so that the crew did not revert to their old habits. Over time, the crew accepted the fact that they were Navy guys, albeit working men, and began to take pride in doing things the Navy way. They also overcame their resentment of the mean old XO.

In port, the men were required to be in the uniform of the day, which was usually Navy issued chambray work shirts and dungarees with white hat. Dress uniforms were required only for those standing quarter deck watch, or during a scheduled ceremony onboard the ship.

At sea, the uniform changed drastically. Unlike larger ships, and what we considered to be non-working Navy ships, the uniform for everyone on the Ute became more casual if we were not entering a port or operating with other ships, which was most of the time. The enlisted guys were allowed to wear t-shirts and dungaree shorts. The officers, including the CO and XO, could also wear tee shirts and khaki pants or shorts. The exception was the watch section personnel on the bridge, who were required to be in regular uniform. The first time I saw this relaxing of uniform standards while underway, I really did not know what to think. But when I saw the Captain on the bridge in a clean white tee shirt and khaki pants, I became a convert. When you think about it though, it made sense. Our sailors were working on deck tending to maintenance of the ship, and often a tow, in horribly uncomfortable tropical temperatures and humidity. They became filthy, hot, and tired, so why not make them a bit more comfortable by letting them wear cooler clothing? After that, even I could be found on the bridge in a tee shirt, khaki pants, and a pair of brown Wellington boots. Casual attire was one thing, but I had to constantly be on the prowl for the guys who abused this privilege and let their appearance become too shaggy or dirty.

The Ute Spirit

Tying into the Ute's hull number, 76, the ship's plaque depicted a Ute Native American war bonnet, with the ship's motto of "Spirit of 76." The inference, of course, was that the ship and crew would demonstrate the same strength, fortitude, and character of the individuals who had guided our fledgling nation in 1776. Obviously, this included a "can do" attitude, which is exactly what was always demonstrated by the unsung heroes of the Ute. No matter what the job or challenge, the men of the Ute would give their utmost to achieve the necessary goal.

The military, and specifically a small Navy ship, is a huge social leveler. The poor kid and the rich kid come together in close confines and become equals. The liberal and conservative; the white, the black, the brown, the yellow; the Protestant and Jew; all become brothers-in-arms. They all must get along to achieve the goal. This is much like a sports team. All must function as a team to achieve the proper results. What took place in a young man's life prior to coming aboard the Ute, really did not matter. The team is what mattered on the ship. Men became very close friends and looked out for one another. They kept one another safe from harm. They did not lie, and they did not steal from each other. They respected each other and treated each other accordingly. Each individual had a job to do on the ship. If you shirked your duty, or did not give it your best work, you hurt the other members of the team, which in turn, hurt the ship. If you hurt the team and/or the ship, an individual could be seriously hurt or killed in the dangerous work of the ship. If you did not pull your weight, the senior enlisted members would let you know and "counsel sternly" when required.

When I observed the men as they worked, I was always amazed at the camaraderie and the spirit of these young men. The Ute was recognized as a leader among the WESTPAC ATFs, and it was due to the spirit of its fine crew, heroes toiling in obscurity.

Forty-Five Degrees

The Ute was an oddly shaped ship. Although she was over two hundred feet long, she was not shaped like a combatant. A Navy destroyer or cruiser is sleek, fast, and gives the appearance of motion while standing still. Conversely, the Ute had a stubby, high, rounded front bow. Her lines tapered to the stern, which was only about five feet above the surface of the water. The stern was rounded, with a huge set of rollers in the center of stern's aft portion. This set of rollers allowed the large towing cable to run through them and out to any tow that the Ute was pulling. But the stubby shape of the ship, with its fairly shallow draft overall, and the relatively flat bottom of the sternward third of the ship, meant that the ship did not ride well at all. Wait, that is a gross understatement. In any kind of rolling sea, the Ute rode like the devil's own bucking bronco. By virtue of its oddball shape and hull structure, the ship could not slice through the water and waves the way a conventionally shaped sleek ship would. Instead, the Ute wallowed and rolled in the swells like a big fat duck.

At the risk of disagreement from many seasoned mariners, I will make the statement that the South China Sea is one of the roughest bodies of water in the world. Even under normal conditions, the South China Sea is full of rough waves, resulting in heavy rolling conditions for a ship. When Mother Nature churns up the South China Sea with gale force winds, storms, typhoons, and other weather tricks, the sea becomes downright frightening. Most of the Ute's operating time in WESTPAC was spent in that sea, as we made our transits from Subic Bay to Vietnam and other ports bordering the South China Sea. We traveled in numerous storms and rough conditions. In these instances, the poor Ute took a terrible beating. The ship would roll back and forth, as well as rise and fall, on the crest of each huge wave.

During the time I served on the Ute, a series of three pictures of the Ute were taken by an unknown photographer during rough sea conditions from another close-by Navy ship. I remember that the photos appeared in some forgotten Navy publication. In my research I was unable to ascertain the original source of the photos. But I kept copies of those pictures for the past forty years. The first picture shows the Ute's bow completely out of the water as she waddled up over a huge wave. The next picture shows the Ute at a fairly level condition. And the final picture shows the Ute with its bow completely under water as the ship dove down the side of the wave. I have included those pictures in this book, as they portray the powerful forces of nature acting upon our sturdy little ship, and the resultant "ride of our life" that the crew always experienced on the Ute.

A steel rod was welded to the overhead (ceiling) on the Ute's bridge. The rod extended across the width of the bridge, and in really rough weather, some of the bridge crew would literally hang from that bar as the ship rocked and heaved with the waves. We became human pendulums while the ship went through its gyrations under our suspended feet.

A clinometer was located in a prominent place on the bridge. A pendulum was attached to the face of the device, and across the bottom of the face were numbers corresponding to degrees of roll of the ship. As the ship rolled, the pendulum would swing back and forth across the face of the clinometer, with the point of the pendulum pointing to the degree number(s) at the bottom of the instrument. In this way, we could determine the exact roll the ship was taking. It was fairly common for the Ute to take rolls as high as forty-five degrees. Try to imagine that the floor in your house is rolling back and forth at a steady rate of forty-five degrees each way all day and all night long. Now, imagine trying to walk across the floor. Try to imagine carrying out your daily household chores in this house. Try to imagine attending to your toilet tasks. Try to imagine sleeping while your bed rolls back and forth forty-five degrees. And try to imagine sitting down to eat while your house is spinning through the ocean. If you have never experienced such a ride, it is hard to imagine the difficulties of the experience. On the bridge, we kept an eye on the clinometer, and our record roll of the ship was forty-eight degrees. You simply cannot imagine the muscular effort your body exerts while you try to walk, hang on to something, or carry out your normal duties twenty-four hours a day, while the ship is heavily rolling. I guess that is why there were few overweight sailors on the Ute. Although you might overcome your seasickness, you never became accustomed to the ferocious random movements of the ship as it was tossed about on the ocean. The South China Sea was always a dangerous place to be.

The Navigator, Part I

Remember the problems I had with navigation classes while at Officer Candidate School? And the subsequent navigation school I attended en route to the Ute? When I went aboard the Ute, I wondered whether or not I could successfully transition into the ship's navigator role.

The Ute navigation section relied primarily upon celestial navigation. Just like the ancient mariners, we used a sextant to measure the height of celestial bodies at a specific time to determine the ship's position in a huge body of water with no landmarks in sight. To track the ship's position, we took sightings of stars in the morning, stars at dusk, and the sun at noon time. In addition to celestial, the Ute had an electronic radio navigation set called LORAN, model C (Charlie). Even by standards at the time, this particular LORAN gear was considered out of date and unreliable. Therefore, as the ship's navigator, I seldom used that piece of equipment. In transit, far from land, I relied solely on celestial navigation, the very same type navigation I had struggled so hard to learn, with limited success, at OCS. But the Navy course I took *en route* to the Ute was taught in a manner that I easily understood. So as I assumed navigation duties of the Ute, I was ready.

My navigation section included a quartermaster chief, a third class quartermaster, and a quartermaster striker (a sailor under training to be a quartermaster). The chief and I each had our own sextant, and he and I would shoot the stars and sun each day. I think that because my eyes were younger, and with practice, my navigation fixes (the exact spot on the navigation chart designating the ship's location) were tighter than the chief's. The old chief disputed this, so he and I would have a contest at each shooting to see who could have the tightest fix on our individual efforts. Ideally, a really tight fix is when the lines that are plotted on the chart from each star shoot, all intersect at one point. That seldom happens, so the best celestial navigator was the one who had his set of lines intersecting to form the smallest opening between the lines. This small point was the position of the ship on the navigational chart.

The only time that we were unable to use celestial navigation was when the weather was overcast. When we could not see our stars and sun for shooting, we resorted to dead reckoning and the LORAN set. It seemed that neither the chief nor I could ever get an accurate reading from that cantankerous machine, which led to many "best guesses" as to our ship's position. The LORAN set relied on radio waves to receive its signals, and often the ship was simply at the very fringes of, or out of the range of those signals, making the LORAN rather useless.

Of all the jobs I had in the Navy, I enjoyed being the Ute's navigator more than any other. I derived a tremendous sense of satisfaction from being the guy responsible for charting the ship's course over thousands of miles of open ocean. I would rise early in the morning, grab a cup of coffee, and head to the chart house (a little room behind the ship's bridge where our navigation equipment and charts were kept). The chief and I would synchronize our stop watches with the atomic clock in Colorado via world-wide radio, then pick our stars from the ship's navigation reference books. These books identified the most prominent stars and their compass bearings on that date, in the area the ship was operating. Usually, we would have from six to eight stars to shoot. We would then begin shooting the stars with our sextants. While the ship continually rolled around beneath our feet, we would brace ourselves against the bridge wing bulkhead and sight through the lenses. Carefully moving the adjustment screws on our sextants, we measured the angled height of each star from the horizon and marked the exact time of our readings. Accurate readings necessitated our being able to view both the star and the horizon. As we shot each star, the third class quartermaster would keep track of the stop watches and record the figures we read to him from our sextants. After we had shot all of the prescribed stars, we would return to the chart house to complete our sight tables. A sight table is a long, rather complicated form on which several mathematical processes are performed and recorded, along with the sextant readings to create a final figure used to draw an angled line across the navigational chart. Having the resultant lines from each of the six to eight star sightings drawn in the area of the ship's location would ideally result in a point where all of the lines intersected, thus designating the ship's position.

At approximately noon each day, we would shoot the sun. The navigation publications indicated the exact time of day to shoot. It was at this time that the sun would be at its highest angle from the horizon. This exact time was called "local apparent noon." If the sun was shot at this specific time, the sextant reading was entered into another sight table with more mathematical processes to be completed. The result was one line, which was the ship's exact latitude at that precise time. Pretty neat! The same process of shooting stars was carried out again at dusk, when the stars were visible along with the horizon.

I was in awe of celestial navigation and loved it. It was fascinating to me to think of ancient South Seas natives crossing thousands of miles of ocean to settle other islands like Hawaii, or ancient explorers using the same process to find other lands and riches. They looked at the same stars that we used to navigate, even though their methods and instruments would have been considerably more crude. The simple job of being the ship's navigator made me realize that the orderliness, logic, and perpetuity of celestial navigation used by mariners through centuries were a testament to the order of the universe, and helped affirm to me that our harried and chaotic earthly existence is controlled by a tremendously powerful and wondrous force.

Today, ship navigators no longer even think about celestial navigation. Everything is done by Global Positioning Satellites (GPS). Using satellites, a small, hand-held GPS device can tell a navigator the exact latitude and longitude of his/her ship or aircraft to within a small number of feet, at any given time, no matter what the weather. Today's navigators have no idea what they are missing.

Pay Days

One of my administrative duties as the XO was responsibility for all of the personnel records, medical records, and pay records for everyone on board the Ute. With a yeoman and a personnelman to make the actual record entries, there was always a great deal of paperwork on the ship. Entries were made in each crew member's record for any significant change occurring to that individual. New people coming aboard, transferring members, disciplinary results, award and medal notices, change in rate (Navy term for rank), pay changes, marital status changes, and other items all had to be noted in the record. It was a full time job for my two office workers to keep the ship's service records current.

In addition, my ship's office maintained all the pay records. Normally on a large ship, a Supply Corps Officer would have this responsibility. Because we had no true Supply Corps Officer, the administration of pay records fell under the XO's duties. Additionally, on large ships, the crews were paid in cash. That meant that the Supply Corps Officer, designated as the disbursing officer, would make a trip to a bank and come back to his/her respective ship with a bunch of cash. Hence, they were usually armed and had one or two other people in their company. Because we did not have a disbursing officer, we could not pay our crew in cash. They were given checks. Most of the crew would receive fairly small checks, because the bulk of their pay had been automatically deducted and sent home to their wives and families by the Navy. These deductions were called allotments and were set up to ensure that a family would have no financial problems while their sailor was away at sea.

Captain Archie, early on, made it very clear to me that there should never ever be an excuse on my part for our sailors not getting paid on time. As a result, we were never late with pay. At that time, we were paid twice per month. The crew all knew the scheduled pay days. Usually a day or two before pay day, I would take all the crews' pay records to the Subic Bay Naval Base Disbursing Office for that office to print checks for the crew. On pay day, I would return to the disbursing office and pick up the checks. Pay days were always good. Everyone was happy and had money to spend.

When we were scheduled to be at sea for a long period, I had to be sure that pay records were completely up-to-date and deliver them to the disbursing office before the ship left port. The checks would then be waiting for us upon our return. If we were to be gone for an extended period of time and would be stopping at a liberty port after a normal pay day, I could request advance checks to take with us on the ship for distribution on the normal pay day.

In the early morning of pay day, crew members would start asking me what time we would hold payday and hand out the checks. It would normally be some time after lunch. The entire crew would line up outside my little office half-door, and as the sailors each signed a receipt, we began handing out checks. My unsung heroes loved their pay master, and everybody smiled for the entire day.

Strangely enough, I enjoyed the aforementioned administrative duties of the XO on the Ute. In the civilian world, those duties are similar to those of a Human Resources Office in private industry, and I believe that exposure to this work guided me into my vocation in Human Resources and Labor Relations after I left Navy active duty.

The Ute's Vietnam Service

The approximately 75 unsung heroes on the Ute made their service contributions to the Vietnam war through their pure hard work. The ship made its home-away-from-home in Subic Bay. From there we operated throughout the Western Pacific region. The ports of call in South Vietnam were Vung Tau, Cam Ranh Bay, and Da Nang. All three of these locations had established allied military bases, and the Navy operated in each of them. We would be contacted in Subic Bay and ordered to travel to one of the three ports to pick up a tow. Our mission would be to proceed across the South China Sea to Vietnam, pick up disabled or excess American water craft, and tow them back to the Subic Bay shipyard for repairs. Rigging these tows is back-breaking, heavy, dangerous, dirty work. The Ute's unsung heroes never complained and did not shirk their duty. The crew and the riggers carried out their work like the professionals they were. We were always aware that our work helped the front line units do their jobs, and we always wanted to help in any way we could. We made countless trips back and forth to Vietnam from Subic. Some examples of our tows included Yard Water Ships, Yard Oilers, Mines-weepers, and floating cranes. Yard water ships and yard oilers are small-er-sized ships that can bring their cargo of fresh water or petroleum products into a harbor for use by the personnel in that port. Their size permitted them to enter almost any port and tie up at a pier. In one of our return trips to Subic, three of these small ships were secured to our tow gear, trundling along in our wake as we made our way back to the Phil-ippines. On another trip, we also had three ships being towed behind us, and one of those ships was an MSO. How ironic; I had served on MSOs for two years, never leaving Charleston, and this MSO was seeing duty sweeping for mines off the coast of Vietnam. But the old temperamental non-ferrous diesels on the MSOs were notorious for breakdowns, and this one was living proof as we towed her back to Subic. We looked like a momma duck with all the little ducklings following along in our wake. Ute's top speed was only about fourteen knots, and when we had large tows our speed might drop to nine knots. So our trips back to Subic re-quired from four to six days transit, depending upon the weather and load we were pulling.

I emphasize that the Ute was a non-combatant service ship, and we really would have had trouble if we had been attacked. In all of our trips to South Vietnam, only one incident raised an alarm. On that particular trip, we had just arrived in Cam Ranh Bay and were working with the Navy Sea Bees, another group of unsung heroes, to start rigging our tow. Suddenly above the hills of the Cam Ranh Bay base facility, Viet Cong rockets began to be fired toward the base. Our rigging crew immediately broke the towing gear apart, and Captain Archie quickly got the Ute un-derway and steamed out of the harbor and out of harm's way. It is highly unlikely that any of the rockets would have come close to us at the base piers, nor would our little humble ship ever be considered a worthy tar-get, but we waited out the enemy attack off-shore, returning to the harbor after the fireworks were over. We then completed preparation of our tow and headed to sea. That was as close to any conflict that I or the Ute ex-perienced while I was aboard. We certainly were not the tip of the spear.

On several of our trips into Vietnam, the ship would have to wait in the harbor or just outside the harbor while personnel in port prepared our tow. We would drop anchor and wait, sometimes for as long as twenty-four to forty-eight hours until the tow was ready for us. When we anc-hored in Vietnamese waters, we always set up a security watch. This consisted of two roving sailors with rifles, one on the bow and one on the stern of the ship, to watch for approaching boats or swimmers, and a third look-out with binoculars on the bridge. This usually resulted in nothing more than several hours of boredom.

Spooky Boxes

The Navy Seal—A college professor, an avowed atheist, was teaching his class. He shocked several of his students when he flatly stated he was going to prove there is no God. Addressing the ceiling he shouted, "God, if you are real, then I want you to knock me off this platform. I'll give you ten minutes. The lecture room went silent. You could have heard a pin drop. The ten minutes was nearly gone when the professor taunted God, saying, "Here I am God! I'm still waiting." At the last second, a Navy Seal, just released from active duty and newly registered in the class, walked up to the professor and punched him full force in the face. The professor was out cold before he hit the floor. The students were all in shock. The Navy Seal took his seat in the front row and the class waited. Eventually the professor came to. When he could finally talk, he glared at the Navy Seal in the front row and asked, "What's the matter with you. Why in the world did you hit me?" The Navy Seal smiled, and replied, "God was busy. He sent me."

—Author unknown

Immediately after we had docked on one trip into Da Nang, two Navy Seals, an officer and an enlisted man, came aboard the ship and asked if they could look around. Of course, we were in awe of these two guys. We had heard innumerable stories about Navy Seal exploits and bravery in the face of overwhelming odds against the enemy. The two men thoroughly inspected the ship, thanked us, and went back onto the pier. In a few minutes, the personnel who would give us our tow came aboard for conference. It was then revealed to us that we would not be hitching up a tow. The Seals had been scouting the Ute to ensure that we had room for our soon to be received cargo, and also confirming we had no foreigners on board.

At various times, we hosted one or two South Vietnamese officer trainees. They would ride the ship and observe U.S. Navy practices in navigation and conning the ship. They were always friendly and interested in our work, but could seldom speak fluent English. Additionally, the guys were almost always seasick. Between not speaking the language and spending time in their bunks due to seasickness, I am not sure how valuable their training with us was. The Seals were, no doubt, ensuring that none of the South Vietnamese trainees were on board for this trip.

The cargo we would be carrying back to Subic soon arrived on the pier. It consisted of two small, portable, windowless buildings. They were craned onto the fantail of the Ute, lashed together, and securely tied down to the deck. It was later revealed that these were "spook shacks." The shacks could be placed in various locations of the combat theater to monitor North Vietnamese communications and also could be used as secure locations in which to store gathered intelligence. The shacks had been sealed before they were placed on our deck, and we were instructed not to open them. For a couple of non-descript gray metal box sheds, everyone seemed to be giving them a lot of attention. It was almost as if they were not sure that our frumpy-looking little Navy ship was capable of this "important" mission.

When the last of the preparations had been completed, the cargo was signed over to us, and we, once again, headed into the South China Sea. As the first of the swells of a pending storm began rolling the ship, our deck personnel made a final extra lash-down of our cargo, and we churned our way through the rolling and pitching sea to Subic. We were met in Subic Bay by yard tugs with "extra interested" personnel, who came aboard the Ute prior to docking. After we were secured at the pier, a whole gaggle of folks swarmed around and watched as those sheds were craned off the Ute and turned over to their recipients. Thank goodness we were rid of this high interest cargo. Little did we know that we would see those ugly little sheds again at a later date.

Gunnery Practice

The Gunnery Chief was watching the lead gunner's mate taking firing practice. He couldn't hit the broad side of a barn, and ended up with a horrible score. He walked over to the chief and said disgustedly, "I think I'm going to commit suicide by shooting myself." "By shooting?" said the chief, "Not a bad idea, but you better take lots of bullets!"

—Author unknown

The Ute possessed a bit more firepower than the MSOs. We had an open-mount, three-inch fifty caliber gun on the bow of the ship, and two fifty caliber machine gun mounts just aft of the bridge. The three-inch was another of the manual type guns, which required the gun crew to use hand cranks to raise, lower, and pivot the gun to acquire a target. Bottom line, on a pitching rolling ship like the Ute, we would have been lucky to hit the broad side of a barn. But we continued to hold periodic gunnery training, firing the three-inch mount and the fifty calibers. The machine guns were fun to shoot; they made lots of noise and could spit out shells at a very rapid rate. Many of our empty fifty-five gallon oil drums saw duty as targets for our gunnery practice. A fifty caliber shell is a formidable projectile, and the velocity is exceptional. As a result, a fifty caliber machine gun can do an extensive amount of damage in a short time. Two or three well-placed shots at a floating barrel would quickly dispatch that pesky barrel to the bottom of the sea.

On the other hand, the three-inch cannon was an unwieldy monster. If a person stood beside the three-inch mount as it was fired, the shock wave would stun his whole body. When I stood next to the mount, it felt like my heart had stopped with each shot. It would take five to ten seconds for my ears to readjust to hear again, and several hours before normal hearing returned. Remember, no ear plugs back then when firing guns. Previous crews on the Ute, especially in World War II, and also in Korea, used the three-inch mount quite often. In my research on the Ute, I found that the ship and its gun were used for shore bombardment in the Aleutian Islands during World War II, and again in the Korean conflict.[24] However, for us, the three-inch mount was a whole lot of weight the ship carried around for not much purpose.

During one of our gunnery practices, an accident occurred with one of the fifty caliber machine guns. A group of sailors and officers were standing around the starboard mount and taking turns firing at floating targets. One of the young sailors stepped up to the gun and began firing it. For some unknown reason, the gun misfired and sent a piece of the shell casing shrapnel shooting backwards into the chest of the sailor. He stumbled back and slumped to the deck, gasping for breath. When we laid him on his back and opened his shirt, we could see a large black piece of metal under the skin, next to his sternum. He was breathing all right and in minimal pain, but the shrapnel piece was in his chest. Apparently, the metal had entered with such force and speed that there was literally no bleeding. The Ute did not carry a doctor, but we had a first class Hospital Corpsman. He examined the wound and decided that it was beyond his expertise. We simply did not know how seriously the young man was injured, nor how deep the metal extended into his chest. At the time, we were half-way between Vietnam and Subic, so we were at least three days transit from a doctor. We radioed Subic and advised the fleet staff of our situation. They later contacted us to report that based on our position, a helicopter would try to locate us. Within two hours the helo arrived, and while we slowed the ship to a stop, the helo hovered over the fantail. A basket was lowered from the aircraft, but the wind was so strong that the basket was swinging to and fro and was very unst-

[24] Navy History, USS Ute ATF-76, http://historycentral.com/navy/aircrafttenders/Ute.html.

able. The helo was running low on the fuel needed for its return flight to Subic, so our crew made valiant efforts to quickly snare the swinging basket. The crew was able to finally grab the basket, and the injured sailor was lifted into it. The helo crew winched the basket into their chopper and swiftly headed out of sight. We were all relieved to later learn that the injury to the sailor was minor, and the piece of metal had not entered any organs. It was stopped by the young man's sternum and ribs and was easily removed and stitched. He was fortunate as it could have been much more serious.

Speaking of the Corpsman

The ship's corpsman was part of the XO's organization on the ship, and therefore, he reported to me. In addition to the corpsman, the ship's yeoman and personnelman both reported directly to me. The corpsman was a first class petty officer, senior in his rating. He was certainly not a doctor, but because of his expertise, he was considered the ship's expert in Navy first aid and medical procedures. He and I got along well, and he confided in me regarding the medical condition of the men and the hygienic conditions aboard the ship. As you can imagine, with seventy sailors having liberty in Olongapo on a regular basis, certain medical issues occurred rather frequently. The corpsman and I gave periodic lectures to the sailors regarding safe sex, but some guys just didn't listen. I had a lot of respect for our corpsman, as I believe that he saw service with the Marines in a front line unit in the course of his career prior to being assigned to the Ute. That respect would change later.

I had noticed a strange growth under the skin on the top of my right arm, near the elbow. It was a small, round, pea-size, ball appearing growth that did not go away, but was ever so slowly growing. I did not worry too much about it, because it did not bother me. It was more of a curiosity item, but I certainly wondered what it was. One day, the corpsman noticed that I was absent mindedly rolling that thing under my fingers as I was talking to him. He then said, "XO, let me dig that thing out of there." After much objection on my part, I finally agreed to let him remove it. We went to his little medical office, and I sat down. He then cleaned the area thoroughly and pulled out a scalpel.

"Whoa," I said. "Aren't you going to give me a local anesthetic?"

"No, these scalpels are brand new and so sharp that you won't even feel it," he said.

Wrong—I felt it! But he was right in the sense that it didn't hurt as much as I had thought it would. I looked away as he cut the little pea sized cyst out of my arm and then put three stitches in the incision. When

I told Captain Archie about this episode, he added it to the other items on the, "Why the XO is crazy" list, and shook his head.

My respect for the corpsman took a huge nosedive later. The corpsman had received orders and would soon be transferred off the ship to another command. I kept part of the ship's supply of medical narcotics in my personal safe located in the ship's office. As I recall, there were about six different bottles of pills and two bottles of alcohol that were locked in the safe. In one of my weaker moments, and because the pills were to be prescribed by the corpsman, I gave him the combination of that safe. I put my trust in him.

As part of the process of the corpsman's transfer, a formal inventory of the items in sick bay and my safe was required. We completed the inventory, and in a few days, the corpsman left the ship for his new duty station. Shortly thereafter, I had occasion to open the safe and then noticed that two bottles of pills were missing. Now this was a huge, oh crap, moment. Those drugs were on a controlled substances list and had to always be accounted for. And I was responsible. I immediately reported my finding to Captain Archie. After he blew his top at me, chewed me out, and told me how stupid I was, he cooled down, and we called the Naval Investigative Service (NIS), the precursor to today's NCIS. Two agents were dispatched to the ship. They searched the ship and thoroughly pored over our controlled items lists, and then proceeded to grill me for hours. I did not take the pills, and I did not know where they were. I also informed them that I had given the combination to my safe to the corpsman, who had recently been transferred. The end result of this fiasco was that NIS could not determine where the drugs had gone nor who took them. Hence there were no consequences, other than them also telling me how stupid I had been to share that safe combination.

I had trusted another human being to be honest and ethical. I rued my naiveté. But to this day, I suspect I know what happened to those pills. To my knowledge, only two people had the combination to that safe, and I did not abscond with the pills. I tell my family all the time that most of the lessons I have learned in life have been learned the hard way. And many times that method of learning is costly. This was another example.

The Druggies

Much has been written about the rampant illegal drug use by the front line soldiers in Vietnam. Some of this unbridled journalism and reporting would make a reader believe that every military man or woman in Vietnam was an illegal drug user. I tend to disbelieve most of this talk. I can truthfully say that I have never used or even experimented with any illegal drugs in my entire life. Yes, I may be an anomaly, but because of my perspective, I find it very hard to believe that a young man who is going into a potentially life threatening fire fight with enemy soldiers would want to be under the influence of judgment and reflex-hindering drugs. But I am also not so naïve to believe that drugs were not a problem in the military of the Vietnam era. And the problem was not just on the front line. Many of the Navy ships and commands also had their share of drug abusers. The Ute was no exception. I was fairly certain that we had two users on our ship, and therefore, we may have had a couple more. One of these guys was a radarman, a fairly skilled and responsible position. Radarmen keep a vigil on the ship's radar scopes to ensure the ship's safety during port entry navigation and at sea to prevent the ship from approaching other ships in its vicinity. For this reason, and others, I did not want a radarman who was using drugs. I kept a close eye on our two suspects, but could never catch them in the act. At one point, Captain Archie and I had the NIS come to the ship and conduct a search. They also interrogated those two knuckleheads; also to no avail.

A new eighteen-year-old sailor reported aboard who was a radarman striker. Because of this, he would be working closely with the aforementioned radarman. I had interviewed the young man when he came aboard, and he was a nice kid from Minnesota. He had one of those Minnesota names that ended in "son" or "sen," like so many Minnesota folks of Norwegian or Swedish ancestry. I'll call him Peterson. I liked this kid, and I kept my eye on him, because I did not want to see him corrupted by our not so stellar, radarman.

One day, while the ship was underway, I was standing aft of the bridge on the portion of the deck above our motor whaleboat. As I gazed out to sea, the two suspected drug users and Peterson walked up to the motor whaleboat and stood to the side of the boat talking. They did not know that I was on the deck above their heads and could see plainly what they were doing. Then I watched as Peterson took something which had been concealed in his hand, and furtively placed it under the tarp covering the whaleboat. After talking a bit more, the three sailors walked away from the boat. I jumped down the ladder to the boat deck and lifted the tarp. I found a short, green, drug smoking pipe, which had evidence of prior use. I took it to the bridge and showed it to Captain Archie. I told him I wanted to keep it for a while, and I locked it in my cabin safe.

The next day, I saw Peterson and I told him I wanted to talk with him in my cabin. He came in and sat on my bunk while I sat at my desk. I didn't say anything, and the poor kid was scared to death. No one wanted to be called to the XO's cabin. I got out of my chair, dialed the combination on my safe, opened it, and pulled out the drug pipe.

Then I said, "I found your pipe."

Now he was scared to death and was visibly shaking, but he denied it was his. I told him I had observed him put the pipe in the whaleboat. I thought he would wet his dungarees. I then went into lecture mode and told him I did not want to see him go down the same road as his comrades, and I thoroughly chewed his behind. He was on the verge of tears. Next I pulled out the big gun to a green eighteen year old. Coming from the same general area of the country as he did, I knew the common family dynamics of folks in the upper Midwest. I told him that when we got back to Subic I was going to call his mother in Minnesota and tell her that her son was a druggie. The last of his composure melted away, and he began crying.

"Please XO, don't do that. I don't want my family to know what happened," he said.

We went back and forth like that for a while, but in the end, I think I had his attention. He promised me that he would not associate with those other guys and would keep himself away from any drugs. To my knowledge, he kept his promise, and I had no further reason to doubt him. I often wonder how that young man's life turned out. I certainly hope he kept his word and made his family proud of him.

Later, we once again called in the NIS to ask if they could process the drug pipe for evidence that would implicate my two primary suspected drug users, but they were unable to help us. Even though I had absolutely no respect for the two suspected drug users, as a matter of curiosity, I also wonder how the rest of their lives turned out.

Hong Kong One

Navy ships are always pleased to receive orders from their commanding staff directing the ship to a port for much needed rest and recuperation. The Ute received orders to head for Hong Kong for a ship visit in the fall of the year. Hong Kong is a remarkable place. The old saying goes that if you want something, it can be found and purchased in Hong Kong. The shopping for sailors on liberty was always a good time. Custom made clothing, every imaginable type of electronic gadget, extraordinary jewelry from all over the Far East, and all sorts of hand crafted products could be found. We were met at the harbor entrance by a pilot boat. The pilot climbed aboard and directed the ship into the crowded harbor. He moved the ship to its assigned berthing area, and soon the ship was secured to a pier.

Let me take a minute to explain the term "ship pilot." Every port of consequence in the world has ships' pilots. They are civilian ship drivers who work at that port, assisting vessels unfamiliar with the harbor to safely navigate through the port entrances, sea lanes, and within the port.

In essence, control of driving the ship is handed over to the pilot when he comes onto the bridge. He gives the helm orders to the crew and drives the ship to its assigned berth. The ultimate responsibility for the ship, however, never leaves the Captain. Based on his intimate knowledge of the harbor, the pilot's recommendations are almost always followed, but the Captain can always overrule the pilot if he thinks his order is in the best interest and safety of the ship. It is a unique relationship in the nautical world.

I was excited to have the opportunity to experience Hong Kong. Because this was my first visit to the city, LTJG Rob, and ENS Adam accompanied me as we went sightseeing. We played tourist for a couple of days and visited every point of interest in the city. We had a great time, and I did a lot of shopping for Jan and for our house, acquiring jewelry and many articles that we still have in our home today. On the third day, I went on a quest with ENS Adam.

I am an old motorcycle guy who has driven motorcycles since I was fourteen years old. (Ok, ok, not legally at that age, but I did it anyway.) I had heard from other Navy guys that a motorcycle could be purchased in WESTPAC at a considerable savings as opposed to the prices in the states. Armed with this knowledge, I was in the market for a new Yamaha 350 cc two-cycle motorcycle—allegedly one of the hottest bikes on the road at that time for its size.

Off we went, to find a Yamaha motorcycle shop in Hong Kong. Asking dozens of Chinese people for directions and going through labyrinths of narrow back streets, we went deeper and deeper into the city, to areas where we received some very curious looks, some of which seemed a bit unfriendly. We had no idea where we were going and were sure we would never find our way out of there again. Finally, we stumbled upon a little hovel in the wall that had a dingy, rusted Yamaha sign hanging in front of it. I was convinced that this could not be the place, but we went in. I began talking to one man, and he quickly ran in the back and returned with another man who spoke broken English. I continued talking with the second man, and he assured me that he was a bona fide Yamaha dealer. I was understandably skeptical. He then took me into the jumbled back storage and repair area of the shop. I honestly did not believe that this could be a viable retail business. In appearance, it was unlike any reputable motorcycle business in the states. There were motorcycles strewn about the room in various stages of repair, or disrepair. And there were unopened boxes of parts and new motorcycles.

I explained what I was looking for and asked him if he had the model I wanted. He said no, but he could get it in one day. So, we began haggling over a price. I knew what the motorcycle sold for in the states, so I wanted a much better price. We haggled for several minutes, and we both enjoyed jabbing each other. We finally agreed to a price which was, indeed, less than the price charged in the states. It was time for me to take a great leap of faith and put my trust in this little, old Chinese man. I paid him half of the agreed upon price, and he said he would deliver the new bike in its crate to the ship the next day. I knew it was possible that I would never see him again, and I had just given him rather a lot of money.

But sure enough, in the late afternoon of the following day, his little delivery truck arrived on the pier with the brand new motorcycle still in its crate. A couple of our ship's deck crew fired up the ship's fantail winch, hoisted the crate up to the upper deck of the ship, and tied it down to ensure that it would ride out the stormy seas back to Hawaii. I paid the dealer the rest of his money, and we exchanged a few pleasantries before he headed back to his shop. I looked into the new crate through the slats in the sides of the crate. The motorcycle and all its parts were packed in heavy clear plastic, and I could see the motorcycle was in many pieces for shipment from its Japanese manufacturer. I would have fun putting that bike together after we returned to Pearl Harbor.

Our stay in Hong Kong was soon at an end, but I had enjoyed it so much that I decided if I returned to Hong Kong during our next cruise, I would have Jan meet me there so she could also enjoy the experience.

Primo

Remember, I alleged that almost anything that a person would want could be purchased in Hong Kong? That even includes living things. About a day after the ship left Hong Kong on its way back to Subic, while making my morning rounds, I ventured down to the crew's berthing area. As I stepped into the space, I glanced down at the deck to check the neatness and cleanliness. What the hell was that? It looked like animal excrement, and upon closer examination, that is indeed what it was. I noticed four of the sailors crowded down on their hands and knees in a corner of the deck. I thought they might be playing cards or something, so I walked closer. They were looking at me, but trying to hide something behind them. I asked them what they had, and they sheepishly pulled out a brown, fuzzy puppy. A dog—the last thing we needed on the ship was a dog. They had conspired with a few of their buddies to buy the dog from a street peddler, and they then smuggled the critter on board before we left Hong Kong. The four of them ganged up on me, pleading and asking if they could keep the dog on the ship as a mascot. Now, I am a real dog lover, but I did not want a dog on the ship, period. The Ute was an unusually dangerous place for humans to live, let alone having to look out for a ball of fur to stumble over. I told them I did not like their idea, but I would not say no. I would ask the Captain, and whatever he decided would be the final word.

Later that day, I told Captain Archie about the dog. He just stood there looking at me as if I had lost my mind.

"Where the hell is this damn dog," he asked.

I told him it was in the crew's quarters, and we both went down there to see the dog. We looked at the pup, and I had to admit, he was a cute guy. He was all brown fuzz, with black ears and a curly tail. And with a half purple tongue, he probably had some Chow in his undoubtedly colorful lineage.

Captain Archie stood there looking at the dog, and he finally turned to me and said, "If I ever step in any dog shit or dog pee on the deck of my ship, I will personally throw that damn mutt over the side. Is that understood?"

I replied, "Yes sir!"

Captain Archie then stomped out of the crew's quarters. I turned to the dog conspirators and said, "Well, you heard the skipper. And guess what—that goes double for me, and I will help the CO toss that flea bag over the side. Keep it out of our sight and make sure you have someone assigned to clean up after him at all times. By the way, what's its name?"

They replied that they had named him Primo. As some of you will know, that is the name of a popular Hawaiian beer. So Primo became a member of the Ute crew. He pretty much had free roam of the ship, but the bridge and eating areas were off limits to him. The crew fed him scraps from their chow. He finally bonded with about four guys on the ship and did not have much interest in anyone else. Frankly, I believe the crew taught that dog that khaki uniforms (worn by the officers) were a threat and should be avoided at all costs. The dog never warmed up to any of the officers on the ship.

One of Primo's buddies was a leading radioman petty officer, so the dog spent a lot of time in the radio room. Every time I walked into the radio room, that stupid dog would growl at me and hide in a corner. Another of Primo's buddies was one of the ship's petty officers who worked in the ship's office—another of the places I spent a great deal of time. When I would enter the office, the dog would growl and slink under the yeoman's desk. As long as he stayed off my radar, I did not really pay much attention to him. The crew loved having the dog on board. They took good care of the little guy, and he became quite the sailor. When really rough weather threw the ship around, he became a bit seasick and found a secluded place in the crew's quarters to curl up and ride out the storm. While we were in port in Subic, he would ride in the ship's pickup truck to go get the ship's mail or radio traffic. He liked riding in the truck with his buddies. Primo also attended some of the baseball games with the team and was a real curiosity item to other ships' crews. The Ute may have been the only ship in WESTPAC that had a ship's mascot dog. I never saw any others.

Once in a while, our Service Squadron Commodore would come aboard to visit and meet with the officers. We did not want to press our luck regarding the presence of a dog onboard, so the crew was under strict orders to hide the dog whenever any senior officers came aboard the ship.

One day the Commodore came aboard to have lunch with the wardroom and look over the ship. Primo was safely hidden away, or so I thought. After lunch, the Commodore, Captain Archie, and I went up to the bridge for a smoke and were standing there chatting. The Commodore was facing toward the front of the ship, and I was facing him and could look over his shoulder to the decks below. I was gazing down to the mess deck level (the main deck), when all of a sudden through the open water tight door of the mess decks, Primo hopped out on to the visible weather deck. The Commodore snuffed out his smoke and was about to depart, so he began to slowly turn around. Then things went into slow motion mode, as things do in a crisis or shocking event. The Commodore continued to slowly turn, but while he was turning, the slow motion scenario continued, and one of the crew appeared to be slowly flying through the air as he sprang through the same water tight door Primo had used. The crew member landed on his feet, scooped up Primo, and pivoted to face the stern of the ship, thereby hiding Primo from the Commodore's view. Real time action resumed, and the crew member nonchalantly walked around the corner on the fantail. Primo's jump out of that door may have led to his eviction if he had been seen by the Commodore. Luckily, we did not have to find out, and he continued to live on his own personal houseboat.

I have no idea what ever happened to Primo, but my guess would be that after several years and a continued good life as a seagoing cur pup, he probably adopted one of the guys and returned home with him to happily live out his retirement from the Navy. We should all be so lucky.

What Island?

The Ute was fortunate to be chosen to be an ambassador ship for a visit to the island of Taiwan. We would be visiting the port of Kaohsiung, Taiwan, which would be a real treat for the Ute, because at that time, very few American Naval Ships were allowed into Taiwan.

One of my tasks as the ship's navigator was to plot the course for the ship to follow as we travelled in the Western Pacific. For each journey, a course was drawn out on navigational charts. These charts were then shown to the captain for his approval. The captain would literally sign off on the journey's course by placing his initials on the charts. The charts with the courses for Taiwan were shown to Captain Archie, and he signed off on our route. I pointed out that on this course, we would be able to use a small island as reference as we passed it on our way to Taiwan. The uninhabited island was actually a rock, no more than a mile in diameter, and a couple hundred feet high—just enough to be a navigational hazard.

We were on our way to Taiwan, and everything was going well. Sure enough, the small island that we were to use as a navigational aid passed about five to ten miles off our port side one evening as we continued on course to Taiwan. The next morning in the Seventh Fleet radio traffic, there was mention of a U.S. ship that had invaded communist China's territorial waters. The identity of the U.S. violator ship was not known. The Chinese government was making a huge diplomatic issue of this incident, and the U.S. government and the Navy were hastily trying to track down a perpetrator. If it were found that no U.S. Navy ship had been in China's territorial waters, then an official denial would be sent to the Chinese. On the other hand, if the event was true, an apology would need to be extended. The flurry of message traffic among the fleet was at a fever pitch. Later that day, we received more messages, and the location of the alleged violation was now issued by the Chinese. I then heard over the ship's PA system, "XO and Quartermaster Chief, report to the Captain's cabin." Oh, crap! That could only mean a problem. The CO almost never summoned me to his cabin. The chief caught me before we went into the CO's cabin and asked me what it was about. I told him I was not sure, but I had a hunch. We went in to see the Captain.

The Captain said, "With all this radio traffic regarding the Chinese island, I want to make sure that we were not the violating ship. Did we go by any islands that might have belonged to the Chinese?"

I told him I was not sure, but that we had used one small island for our navigation purposes. He then told the chief to go to the chart house and bring him our charts showing our ship's course the past two days. When he got these, he studied them for a minute, found the name of the island we had used and the chewing began! Captain Archie kept up our ass-chewing for several minutes, and then he asked the $64,000 question.

"Did I see this course you had laid out for our transit to Taiwan?"

I then showed him his initials on the chart, signifying that he had seen the course, and I had even pointed out the alleged island that we had used for navigation reference. The responsibility then shifted, but the ass kicking continued. I think he was as angry with himself as he was with the chief and me. MUCH later, we all cooled off and began trying to salvage a proper answer to Seventh Fleet staff. When we carefully studied the charts again, it turned out that the nationality of the "owners" of the island was not specified on the chart. Usually a land mass, especially an island, is marked on navigational charts with a small annotation designating the sovereignty of the land. This particular island was not marked on the chart we were using. In addition, on our course, we were far enough from the Chinese Island to be in international waters, but apparently the Chinese did not agree and had started this puffed-up international incident. The Chinese are certainly as adept at navigation as we are, and I have a feeling this incident arose because the Chinese could tell from tracking us that we were headed for Taiwan. I also believe that because they would prefer that the U.S. stay away from Taiwan, they used our passage as a catalyst for their own politics. After a whole lot of groveling and message traffic from us to our fleet bosses, someone way up the food chain made a proper conciliatory response to the Chinese, and the issue was, at last, closed. But not before another difficult lesson was learned by yours truly. In the future I would err on the side of caution and make darn sure we were much farther from any land mass being used for our navigation purposes, especially when the ownership of the land mass is unknown. Captain Archie and the Ute certainly did not need any more of that type of embarrassment. But there was always a tomorrow.

The Taiwan Incident

Not so bright Sailor Johnnie was brought before the CO at Captain's Mast. After hearing all the evidence, the CO said, "I'll give you your choice; one month's restriction, or twenty days' pay." Johnnie responded, "Great, I'll take the pay!"

As I mentioned before, the Ute was fortunate to be one of the few ships to make a port call in Taiwan. The number of U.S. Navy ships that had visited the island nation was small, because of the very tenuous relationship our nation had with mainland China. Remember, this was still during the cold war period, and we did not have the same relationship with China that we have now. For the same reason, it was generally noncombatant type ships which were allowed to visit Taiwan. The U.S. certainly did not want to be seen as rattling sabers by sending in a large warship to a nation that the Chinese still considered part of their empire. That allegation is still true today. China considers Taiwan to be part of the greater nation of China, and they believe that someday this renegade nation of Taiwan should be returned to the communist fold.

Captain Archie and I held several meetings with the crew to caution them to be strictly on their best behavior in Taiwan. They were to be ambassadors of the U.S. government, and they were not to do anything to embarrass the ship or our government. The merchants and bars in Kaohsiung were eagerly awaiting our little band of seventy-five sailors to hit the beach. Prostitution at that time was legal in Kaohsiung, licensed and policed by the government; a much better situation than back in Subic, and the sailors were looking forward to their shore time in Taiwan to do what sailors do. Captain Archie and I met with the local officials to discuss our visit. The big event while the ship was in port was to be a gala banquet hosted by the local government officials, the Taiwan local navy, and other dignitaries. It was to include all of the exotic food and drink anyone could want, followed by speeches and a large floor show. We were all looking forward to it.

The big event would be held on the evening following our arrival. Everyone, except the duty section, gathered at a local hotel's banquet room. As soon as everyone arrived and was seated at the banquet tables, speeches were made with reciprocation by Captain Archie. Next, it was time to eat. The food began to be distributed to all the tables, and it was a feast. There was course after course of mostly dishes with which none of us were familiar. But the sheer volume of food and the flowing alcohol put everyone in a jovial mood. We sampled all of the various dishes, wines, and beers, and for the most part they were all delicious.

At one point, a huge, whole baked fish on a platter was brought to our table. Several of the locals were at our table, and they began some sort of discussion among themselves. An interpreter then explained that the Taiwanese were wondering who would have the honor of eating the eyeball of the fish; considered to be a delicacy. I was not about to join that conversation. I may eat a lot of fish, but I draw the line at various fish parts, and eyeballs would fall into that non-edible category with me. After more discussion, one of the young sailors at the table was given the honor by the hosts. With reluctance, he skewered out the fish eyeball and with a mouth full of beer, he washed down the delicacy, but visibly showed that he enjoyed no part of it. Apparently his style was not considered the best of form by our hosts, but they laughingly applauded the young man. We greatly enjoyed our dinner and conversation, and with stuffed bellies, and a bit too much alcohol consumption, we were now looking forward to the anticipated floor show.

Everyone left the banquet tables and enjoyed a smoke while visiting with our hosts. The dining tables were removed from the banquet room and replaced with rows of chairs from which everyone would observe the floor show. I had no idea what the floor show would be, but I had heard that there were to be some native Chinese dancers and music.

We all took our seats, and the lights dimmed. Sure enough, the Chinese music started with a small group of musicians in one corner of the room. Then, characters in native costumes began to appear, and it was explained to us that this was a silent play, with musical accompaniment, the gist of which was explained to us. The costumes and the music were beautiful, and before too long, the play ended. At this point there was an intermission, and we stood up, smoked with our guests, and got refreshers at the bar.

Soon, we were to take our seats again for the next phase of our entertainment. Once again the lights went down, and the music began. This time, the costumed dancers were all women, and they lined up across the front of their stage and began their dances. After a few minutes, the music tempo picked up, and the tune began to resemble western music. This seemed odd, but even more astonishing, the dancers were keeping up with the music, and they began shedding pieces of their costumes. Of course, the sailors were tuned into this, and nobody's eyes left the dancers. The music turned more into western style rock and roll, and the articles of clothing of the dancers continued to be discarded. Finally, the ladies were wearing only a thin bra and g-strings. Captain Archie and I looked at each other and were somewhat speechless, but of course I cannot say we did not enjoy the show. The music continued, and the sailors became more vocal. They cheered and clapped as the ladies kept up their dancing. Suddenly, the lights went out, and the music stopped. It was pitch black. But slowly the music started again, and the lights came up ever so slowly. As the scene became clearer, it became very evident that the ladies had removed all their clothing and were all dancing in the nude. Well, you can imagine the noise of the sailors. Whistling, clapping, and cheering; they were thoroughly enjoying themselves.

Captain Archie and I were on the edge of our seats—not just because of the show, but because we both knew sailors, and we were watching for the first sign of trouble. And, indeed, trouble began, but not from one of the enlisted sailors. LTJG Rob, who was absolutely reeling drunk, suddenly jumped out of his chair, proceeded to lurch to the front of the room and join the dancing ladies. But to make it even more shocking, he began taking off his clothes—first his shoes; then his socks; then his shirt; then his pants; and then his unmentionables. At this point, he was totally nude, dancing with the girls. The sailors were hooting and hollering and having a big time watching one of their leaders make a complete ass of himself and embarrass the ship.

Captain Archie and I looked at each other briefly, and I jumped out of my chair. I ran over and grabbed the boatswain's mate chief, who also served as our ship's master at arms. I told him to get two or three more guys and grab LTJG Rob and get him the hell out of there, take him back to the ship, and keep him under guard so he would remain on the ship. The chief and his guys grabbed Rob and his clothes and hustled him back to the ship. As you can imagine, the sailors were enjoying all of this and were laughing and cheering the culprit.

By this time the damage had been done, and our reputation as a good will ambassador was in shambles. Captain Archie and I spoke with our hosts and begged them for forgiveness for the boorish behavior of one of our men. Our Taiwanese hosts were very gracious and did not make an issue of the incident. Our gala toned down after that with more music and an open bar. The dancing girls all returned fully clothed and mingled with the sailors. Order had been restored.

The next morning, Captain Archie and I called upon our hosts and took them some mementos from the ship, including ship's plaques and baseball caps. We stayed for a while and chatted with them, drank coffee, and of course, smoked many cigarettes while we chatted. We laughed at the previous night's behavior, and we parted as friends. Shortly thereafter, the ship got underway.

The Commanding Officer of any Navy facility, whether it is ashore, or a ship at sea, has the authority to hear a disciplinary case against an individual in his/her command and decide the appropriate punishment to be levied. This is usually called non-judicial punishment, and the most common methodology for carrying this out is called "Captain's Mast." That afternoon, while underway to Subic, Captain Archie and I held Captain's Mast on LTJG Rob. He was charged with conduct unbecoming of an officer, was monetarily fined, and confined to the ship for the next ninety days. This meant that he would not be able to leave the ship in any port we entered. During my Navy career, I participated in, and was the officiating CO at, several Captain's Masts for enlisted men, but this was the first and only time I ever participated in a Captain's Mast for a Naval Officer. That is a sad commentary in itself.

For some time prior to this incident, LTJG Rob had been very melancholy. He found solace more and more in alcohol and was abusing his liberty time by over indulging each time he left the ship. His alcohol abuse seemed to escalate, culminating in his exhibition at the banquet. Captain Archie severely lectured him during the mast proceedings before he passed sentence, but there was an underlying problem in LTJG Rob's life. Captain Archie told him that happiness would not be found inside a bottle and that only he, Rob, could put his life back on track. This was sad for me, because earlier I had gone on liberty with LTJG Rob many times, and there had been no previous problems. I considered him a friend. But it was apparent that he was having some personal issues which were making it difficult for him to carry out his job as a Navy Officer in an effective and efficient manner. With a Captain's Mast in his record, his career as a Navy Officer was over. When the ship reached Subic, Captain Archie and I arranged that LTJG Rob would be seen by medical and psychiatric staff at the Naval Hospital. Subsequently, LTJG Rob was sent back to Pearl Harbor for convalescence and subsequent permanent transfer off the Ute.

Captain Archie

I have mentioned some of my experiences with Captain Archie. At the beginning of our working relationship, I was very intimidated by this stocky, gruff little CO. But as we worked together more and more, he and I developed a close relationship, and I grew to have great respect for the man. He had come up through the enlisted ranks to become the commanding officer of a U.S. Navy ship. It takes a smart and dedicated individual to do that. Archie had a wealth of experience which I constantly tried to tap into. And yet, he allowed me a great deal of latitude in being his second in command. I conferred with him only on items about which I was uncertain. He would then advise me and let me manage the ship.

The Captain and I would often hold informal meetings while the ship was underway. Our unofficial meeting place was standing at the rail on the deck behind the bridge, and our unofficial meeting times were in the morning following quarters and in the evening after dinner. We were out in the fresh air, enjoying God's wonderful creation, the peace and beauty found in the immense blue sky and sea. Archie might smoke a cigar, and we would talk about anything on our minds. We became close, but Archie was still a somewhat private person, and I seldom socialized with him off the ship. We would go out to dinner together occasionally, but there was always the fine line of military decorum that had to be observed between the commanding officer and a subordinate. That line was less clear when we were standing out along the ship's rail, and I will always remember one of our conversations.

We were standing at our usual informal outdoor meeting place talking, and in the course of our conversation, he turned and looked at me and said, "You know, Jim, when you came aboard I seriously thought that I would end up firing you. You were green as hell, and I thought you would be useless. But you fooled me. You have turned out to be the best XO I have ever seen. I am happy to have served with you, and you can be my XO any time."

Geez, I was speechless, with a lump in my throat. That was the most meaningful thing anybody ever said to me in all my Navy service, and it touched me deeply. I thanked him for his vote of confidence. That remark meant so much to me after I had worked so hard to earn his respect. I will never forget that offhand remark by my commanding officer. Captain Archie continued his career with the Navy, rising in rank, and he went on to command other ships. I ran across his name once in a while; but I finally lost track of him through the years. He was a respected leader of unsung heroes.

Cruise I Wind-Down

The Ute continued its Western Pacific deployment, with the homely little tug carrying out its duties in Vietnam and Subic. We continued to tow target sleds for destroyers' and cruisers' gunnery practice and to pull other ships into the Subic shipyard for repairs. The powerful little ship and its crew of unsung heroes continued to support the front line units. We had been in and out of the Vietnam war zone so often, in fact, that another star was added to the Vietnam Campaign Ribbon which was painted on both sides of the ship near the bridge. We had also spent so much time in the war zone, that the ship earned the Vietnam Service Ribbon. This also meant that each member of the crew also received the same star for his Vietnam Campaign Ribbon, and the Vietnam Service Ribbon which was proudly worn on his uniform. Each of the stars on the campaign ribbon signified different campaigns during which the ship had assisted in the war effort. Our little ship had a proud history and sported several rows of ribbons on the two sides of her bridge level exterior. The various ribbons had been earned through the hard work and sweat of the many individuals who had served on the Ute since her commissioning in 1942. All of these hard working unsung heroes deserved a huge pat on the back for their efforts.

Soon it was time for the Ute and crew to return home to Pearl Harbor. But we had one more order to carry out for the Seventh Fleet Staff. Remember that ugly little spy shack that the ship carried back from Vietnam some weeks before? Well, it returned like a bad penny. We were ordered to once again strap it down to the fantail of the ship and carry it back to Pearl Harbor. When it arrived on the pier, the shack was unceremoniously craned onto the ship and securely lashed down to the deck for its trip back to Pearl. This time there was not nearly the hoopla and concern by various parties that we had seen in Vietnam regarding the security and safety of the shed. I assumed that whatever had been in that shed as we brought it back from Vietnam was removed in Subic, and we were transporting an uninteresting old gray shed back to Pearl Harbor. Just another assignment in the life of a working Navy Service Ship.

Ivan the Stalker

We were released from WESTPAC duty by the Seventh Fleet command and prepared for our departure. The transit back to Pearl Harbor would last well over a week, and we would stop in Guam in transit for provisions and fuel.

As we began our transit to Guam, one morning a ship appeared some miles off our port quarter. The ship remained at that bearing but closed the distance between us. After a day or so of dogging us, the unknown ship finally got to within a couple miles of us, and with binoculars we could make out that the ship was a fishing trawler. Although it had the prerequisite fishing equipment showing on its deck, for some strange reason it bristled with antennae. Captain Archie chuckled at me. He knew exactly what the ship was. He explained to me that trawlers like this were Russian and roamed all over WESTPAC dogging U.S. Navy ships, attempting to intercept communications, but primarily to keep tabs on the movements of U.S. Navy ships. The Russians wanted to know the exact locations of all U.S. Navy ships at all times. This was a common cold war strategy. Captain Archie also speculated that our cargo on the fantail was a curiosity that the Russians wanted a closer look at. What a joke, the spook boxes were empty sheds. As the Russian ship got close enough to us, we sent him a flashing signal light message asking for his identity, knowing full well that he would ignore it. He did. Ivan dogged us for nearly four days before turning around and heading away from us as we got nearer to Guam. Our parting farewell to him was another signal light message to him saying, "Bye Ivan." His response was indecipherable/unrepeatable—must have been in Russian.

All members of the crew were anxious to return to their families whom they had not seen for six months. Each day brought us closer to home. A common practice among Navy ships is to have an "anchor pool." The guys each contribute a couple of bucks and predict a specific day, hour, and minute that the ship would throw over a mooring line and tie up to the home pier with the first mooring line secured to a pier bollard. The sailor who picked the time closest to the actual arrival would win the couple hundred dollars which had been contributed to the pool. Since my navigation section pretty much knew the time that the ship would arrive, we did not participate, and I was made the judge, determining the exact time of arrival.

Even while underway, the crew worked diligently to have the ship looking her best for our arrival. The ship sported some rather rough looking areas where rust was showing, due to our heavy work-load while deployed. When in port, the guys would constantly work to stay ahead of the rust by chipping it off and repainting, but there was always more to be done, some of which was completed on our way home.

By the time we were ready to enter our home port, the crew sported clean haircuts and shaves. The ship looked impressive with its new paint shining and all the brass on the ship gleaming. We were met at the outer buoy of Pearl Harbor by a pilot, who presented us with a huge lei of flowers made by the Ute crew's wives. In Hawaiian tradition, the flower lei was draped around the bow of the ship for its trip into the harbor. The entire crew was dressed in their tropical white uniforms. The little ship and its crew were a sharp looking bunch as we made our way to our assigned pier. We were home at last.

At Home

During the time I was at sea, I missed Janet terribly. I would write to her almost daily. Before I had left Pearl Harbor, I had purchased two portable four track tape recorder/players, so we each had one. At sea, I would record how my days went, where we were, and what was happening on the ship. She would do the same thing in Honolulu, and our tapes would pass each other in the mail. We were then able to hear each others' voices, but it was still a very lonely time while we were separated. In today's modern military, members are able to use satellite telephones and internet to see and hear their families at home.

Jan and the other wives were waiting for the ship on the pier, and as soon as we were able, Jan and I jumped in our car and headed for our house in military housing. Jan had moved into a little junior officer's duplex by the base and had it furnished and decorated. She had been substitute-teaching in the Aiea schools and then had obtained a permanent teaching position at the private Punahou Academy, so she had kept busy while I was gone. It was great to be together and hug each other again.

Leaping Lizards, or How Would You Like Your Eggs?

After being home for a couple days, one morning I was lying in bed with Jan, just waking up. We were both startled to hear a slight rustling noise. The noise would stop, and then begin again. There was a window above our bed's headboard, and we had drapes on the window. The drapes were open, and the soft rustling noise seemed to be coming from near the top of the window. I told Jan that it sounded like we might have a mouse that had somehow managed to get up into the drape. Then we heard a different noise. It was one, small click noise. We really could not figure out what that noise was. So I climbed out of bed to investigate. As I looked around, something on the top of the headboard caught my attention. There on the ledge of the headboard was a tiny egg, about the size of the tip of my little finger. The egg was broken open, and it looked just like a miniscule hen's egg. Now, we were both really curious. Where in the world had this little egg come from? I climbed up and stood on the bed and spotted our intruder. A little greenish tan gecko was sitting nonchalantly on top of the drapery folds giving me the eyeball. I guess she must have been a Ms. Gecko to disturb us with a falling egg. Jan said she had been told by our neighbors that geckos were everywhere in Hawaii, and they were good for catching and eating bugs. They are also nocturnal, so they might make some noises during the night, as they scurried about in their search for a tasty bug to eat. Our in-house geckos were seen occasionally, but we left them alone. Little did we know that one of our geckos might grow up to be a pitch man for an insurance company on television. Smart little lizard.

Parts is Parts

Remember the Hong Kong motorcycle purchase? A few days after returning home, the ship's deck crew transferred the crated motorcycle off the ship and onto the bed of the ship's pickup truck. The crate was transported to our house, and four of us carried it to the back yard of our duplex, after which the other three guys headed back to the ship.

Now my fun would begin. I pried open the crate and soon had all of the motorcycle pieces lying around the back yard. In addition, there were at least a dozen plastic bags filled with various nuts and bolts and parts. Search as I might, there were no instructions on how to assemble all of these pieces to make a new motorcycle. But I was not dismayed; I was confident that I could get this motorcycle put together. Ever so slowly, I opened each of the little bags and spread out all of the pieces so that I could examine them. Jan thought this was a riot; me sitting on the ground surrounded by what appeared to be thousands of motorcycle parts. I worked on that mess for two or three days, and guess what? I assembled all of those pieces, and when I put gas and oil in the motorcycle, it ran, albeit a bit roughly.

There was just one thing I could not figure out. I had put the wiring in, but could not get the tail lights to work. So I rode the motorcycle to the local Honolulu Yamaha shop and asked them to fix the lights and tune the carbs, which they did. Then the manager of the Yamaha shop got a bit belligerent and asked me where I had gotten the motorcycle. I told him I bought it in Hong Kong and brought it over on my ship. I showed him my Hong Kong bill of sale. He asked me that question because the rear turning signal lights were colored red; whereas, the U.S. bikes all have amber turn signals. Perhaps he thought I had illegally smuggled the bike into Hawaii.

I rode the motorcycle to work on the ship every day, and Jan and I would ride it to the beach almost every weekend. We would strap our beach mats to the motorcycle and head down the main highway (at that time it was H-1) to the beach in downtown Honolulu at Army Fort De-Russy. We would spend the day at the beach and then zoom back home. We put a lot of miles on the Yamaha while we were in Hawaii.

Warrant Officer Cobie also had a 350 cc Honda motorcycle of which he was extremely proud. He too, rode his motorcycle to work on the ship every day. Occasionally, after work, he and I would have a drag race on our motorcycles on Kamehameha Highway in Honolulu. So here were two khaki-clad Navy officers who should know better, acting like kids, screaming down the highway to see whose bike was faster. My Yamaha was a two-cycle 350 cc engine, whereas Cobie's was a four-cycle. Because of the power and torque of my two-cycle, I would beat him every time. Cobie hated this because, after all, he was the ship's engineering officer, the top gear-head of the ship. It hurt his pride to be shown up by the XO. We had a lot of fun and for some strange reason, we were never apprehended by the constabulary.

I was not always so lucky with the police though. I had perfected a trick whereby I was able to ride the motorcycle on only its back wheel. By alternately working the throttle and rear brake of the bike, I could ride for blocks with the front wheel in the air. One day on my way home from work, I was riding down our street on the back wheel. Suddenly, from around a corner came a police car. Not only was I riding on one wheel, but I was speeding. I quickly put the front wheel back on the ground, but alas, I had been nabbed. I received a hefty traffic fine for that and learned another in my life's series of expensive lessons.

While at home in Honolulu, Jan and I were able to see my buddy John and his wife again. He had transferred to a second destroyer, the USS Carpenter (DD-825), also home ported at Pearl Harbor. While our respective ships were in the local area, we, along with our wives, were able to get together for dinner and other activities. At that time, John had a genuine British-made Mini Cooper that he loved to drive hard and fast. Jan and I would cram ourselves into the tiny back seat of that "Mini-Coo," and off we would zoom. But true to the quality and performance of British cars of that era, it succumbed to mechanical disaster, and it had to be given its own mini requiem.

It was also during this time at home that I enrolled and completed a certified scuba class so that I could do recreational scuba diving with the Ute's diving officer when we deployed again.

USS Neverbudge

Some weeks after returning to Pearl Harbor in late fall of 1971, the Ute was to go through its annual Refresher Training (REFTRA). The ship and crew would be tested and graded by observers as the ship carried out the various graded tasks. One such exercise involved the simulation of a salvage operation of dragging a ship back into navigable waters after the alleged ship has run aground. The exercise took place in a backwater area, which I believe was a little bay around the back side of Ford Island, the famous island where many of the ships were moored when the Japanese attacked Pearl Harbor during World War II. The Ute steamed to this location and began the exercise.

The first steps were to lower and strategically place our two massive steel salvage anchors. These anchors were at least eight feet tall and would hold the Ute from drifting. They would also give the ship stability while it took a strain on the grounded ship. In the exercise, the grounded ship was simulated by a huge concrete structure which was permanently in place by virtue of having a massive base, which had been buried deep underground. It could never be moved or even be budged. The crew worked feverishly in the tropical sun and soon the anchors were set, and the towing cable was sent across a stretch of water to the "concrete ship." The Ute's towing cable was enormous. It was about the same diameter as a man's arm and was carried aboard the ship on a huge drum at the forward edge of the fantail. This cable was used for all of our ship's towing. The cable was securely fastened to the concrete structure, and the little ship began to take a strain on the cable and the salvage anchor lines. Once the cable was taut, the ship began to turn its screw. Looking over the side of the ship, I could see that we were churning up mud on the bottom of the bay. The orders were given for the ship to increase engine speed. Now, the ship's screw was turning the bay into an ugly, brown, frothing soup from the rapidly turning ship's screw, as the ship strained to move the concrete mass. The ship was ordered to full speed and began shaking violently as every bit of mechanical muscle of the little ship was being put to the test. The bay was now an angry cauldron of flying, brown muddy water. In my mind, all I could see was the danger of the situation. If any of our anchors or cable broke, the snapping and whipping cables could severely damage the ship and wound or even kill a crew member. The ship continued this strain until finally the onboard observer allowed the exercise to cease. The ship and crew had passed the test. Riggers were sent across the cove to unfasten our tow cable, and it was taken back aboard the ship. Next, our salvage anchors had to be retrieved and craned aboard the ship for stowing on the fantail. All went well, and the first anchor was recovered and stowed. The assigned capstan began turning, taking up the slack on the second anchor. But as the anchor chain became taut, the anchor would not budge from the bottom of the bay. This is unusual, because anchors will generally come free from the bottom of the sea with just the power of the capstan pulling it up. But this anchor would not budge. As a last resort, the ship began moving to pull the anchor free. It was feared that taking too much strain on the anchor might break the anchor chain, and the anchor would be lost forever. But soon, the anchor broke its grip in the thick bay mud and was free. It was brought aboard and secured on the fantail. Our REFTRA was completed, and the ship was declared fit for service for another year. Well, maybe not quite yet.

Yards Again

In just a couple of weeks following REFTRA, in late fall of 1971, the Ute was ordered into the Honolulu shipyard for refurbishing and repairs. The ship would have its bottom scraped and repainted, and adjustments would be made to the ship's rudder and steering system, which had been acting up. This condition probably was not helped by that REFTRA exercise I just described. In fact, we thought that the ship's screw had hit something underwater in that exercise which caused some imbalance in the screw.

The yard period would last for approximately six weeks with the ship in dry dock, while a great deal of interior work and painting would also be done. With all of the dirt, toxic chemicals, and vapors used in the overhaul, the crew who normally lived on board could not stay on the ship. The Navy provided a floating berthing barge for the men, located next to the shipyard. The barge consisted of a large berthing area, heads, and several offices. This was to be our home in lieu of the Ute, while the ship was in the yards. Because there was little for the crew to do, this yard period was rather boring for the men. The crew on the barge was responsible for housekeeping and maintenance of the barge, and other tasking to keep them occupied and out of trouble. Vacation leave was granted very liberally so the crew could spend as much time as possible with their families.

New CO

Two major events occurred while the ship was in the yard. I reached my three year anniversary in the Navy and was promoted to full lieutenant.

Those railroad tracks on my collar looked a lot better to me than that little silver bar. The second item was that Captain Archie had reached the end of his tenure on the Ute and received orders transferring him to another Navy command. We would be getting a new skipper. The wardroom organized a going away party for Archie with our best wishes for his continued success at his next duty station. Our unsung hero leader moved on, and I was sorry to see him leave. We had developed a good working relationship, respected, and genuinely liked each other, and now I would have to face another unknown CO.

Lieutenant Ware reported to the Ute as the new commanding officer while the ship was still in the yard, and while we still occupied the barge. Because of my promotion, I was now the same rank as the commanding officer, which I felt was a bit strange, but in a good way. Of course, he was senior to me in time-in-grade and experience.

Lieutenant Ware was very different from Lieutenant Archie. The new captain was a thin, very fit, dark haired and handsome man, who was also an OCS product. Prior to coming to the Ute Captain Ware had served on an ATF, two destroyers, and had attended Navy Post Graduate School. He was very intelligent and grasped the necessary knowledge of the Ute and its operation in short order. He was a Texan, with a rather laid back, southern easiness about him, and I immediately liked him. I enjoyed bringing him up to speed on the nuances of the ship and its crew of unsung heroes. Best of all, he trusted me to manage the ship and keep the ship and crew out of trouble.

Soon the Ute came out of the shipyard and was ready for sea testing to ensure the ship was ready for another deployment. We went to sea for trials, and the old girl sounded just great as her mighty diesels propelled her through the off-shore swells. It was good to feel the ocean's power and the moving ship under our feet again after sitting so long in the yards. The Ute passed her trials with flying colors and was declared ready for sea. We then took up local operation duties off Hawaii, pulling target sleds and carrying out our own exercises to prepare the ship and crew for our future deployment. We also played a lot of baseball, but our star pitcher, Archie, was gone. As a result, our wins became less frequent, but we still had fun.

Driver's Training

A young ensign was given an opportunity to display his ability at getting the ship underway. With a stream of crisp commands, he had the decks buzzing with activity. The ship steamed out of the harbor and soon was at sea. The ensign's

efficiency was remarkable. In fact, he set a new record in get-
ting the ship underway. The ensign glowed with his accom-
plishment and was not at all surprised when a sailor walked up
to him with a message from the captain. He thought it was odd,
though, that it was a radio message. It said, "Congratulations
on completing your underway preparation exercise according
to the book, and with amazing speed. In your haste, however,
you have overlooked one of the unwritten rules. Make sure the
Captain is aboard before getting underway. Now get my damn
ship back here!"

—Author unknown

In the early seventies, most of the Navy ports sponsored ship driving contests. Squadrons of the various ship types would hold competitions to determine who was the best underway OOD of that particular type of ship. The ship drivers in our Pearl Harbor squadron would be competing for the title of "Best Ship Handler" in the squadron for 1971. Captain Ware was new to the ship and did not feel comfortable competing in the contest, so he chose me to drive the Ute. Our squadron commodore, a full commander, would be the judge, and he would ride each ship as it competed.

I have mentioned previously that military protocol was quite different on a small working ship. The crew and officers knew each other very well. An example of that, sometimes casual, relationship could be found in the Ute's very best helmsman (the steering wheel sailor). He was a young Hawaiian native, slender, with coal-black hair, and a thin mustache, and he always had a big grin on his face. He was a good kid, efficient, and followed helm orders better than anyone else on the ship. He had an innate feel for how the ship would react to a helm order and could somehow anticipate how the OOD would respond in a given situation. As a result, he was always at the ship's wheel when we were at sea detail or whenever special attention was needed by the helmsman. Everyone knew this young man well, and he was always called by his nickname— Pineapple. That is what everyone on the ship called him.

The day of the ship handling contest arrived. The gist of the contest was that the OOD would get the ship underway, take the ship out of the harbor, turn it around, return to the harbor, and land the ship at the pier again. The OOD would be graded on his competency in handling the ship without error. I was ready for the fun.

The commodore came aboard the ship, and I methodically and carefully moved the ship away from the pier and headed for sea. Everything had gone exactly right, and it was a perfect show of getting the ship underway. Our primary helmsman, Pineapple, was at the wheel. All the time I was working, the commodore was standing just behind me with a clip board. He did not bother me; I had this stuff down pat. Away we went, to just outside the harbor, where I gave the commands to turn the ship around, and we headed back to the pier. As we approached our specific pier, the helm orders from me were rapid—changes to engine speed and rudder changes came fast and furious as we neared the pier. All the rudder commands to the helmsman were usually preceded or followed by "Pineapple," since he was on the wheel. Example—"Steer three four zero, Pineapple; Mind your helm, Pineapple; Right ten degrees rudder, Pineapple." You get the idea. The ship approached the pier and as we neared it, I reversed the engines of the ship, and the ship engines roared as I ordered the rudder over. The ship's forward motion dropped off and she shuddered to a stop, and I shouted, "All stop, throw over lines one, two, three, and four." The ship became quiet, and stayed in one spot. I had nailed the landing. It was stupendous! The side of the ship was two feet from the pier, at the exact location on the pier, and all lines were being thrown to the line tenders on the pier. It was picture perfect. I glanced over at Captain Ware, and we grinned at each other.

Captain Ware began talking to the commodore, and then I heard the commodore say, "Mr. Duermeyer."

As I walked over to him, I thought for sure he was going to comment on my perfect landing. And he did! "Mr. Duermeyer, that is one of the best ship handling exhibitions I have ever seen. It was an extraordinary effort."

Wow, I was feeling good. But the commodore continued, "But, Mr. Duermeyer, your helm orders leave something to be desired in their lack of professionalism." He continued, "You simply cannot refer to your helmsman as Pineapple. He is to be referred to as Helmsman. Your military demeanor on the bridge is just too lax. Therefore, I cannot give you the ship handling award, even though you are undoubtedly the best ship handler I have seen in the competition."

What a crock of crap! He had a point, but I really didn't agree with his assessment. Even Captain Ware thought I was robbed. Well, in the overall scheme of things, it really was not that important. Our crew knew we did a great job, and everyone on the ship had always called our helmsman Pineapple, so they did not hold it against me for not winning the contest. Pineapple, my unsung hero, helped me look really good that day, though. We filed our loss under "Chicken Shit Technicality," and moved on.

As Christmas of 1971 approached, the CO and I again allowed a liberal leave policy so that the maximum number of crew members could spend time with their families before our upcoming WESTPAC deployment. Jan and I hosted a Christmas party at our home for the Ute wardroom. The festive spirit was evident, and everyone had a memorable time.

Navigator, Part II: Somebody Moved the Island

Just before their first long deployment to the Western Pacific, two ensigns were discussing the stress of leaving their families. A senior officer, a veteran of many deployments, overheard their conversation and offered the following advice: "You must be sensitive to your wives' emotional needs," he said. "Never, ever, whistle while you pack for sea!"

—Author unknown

In January, 1972, the Ute was again sent to the Western Pacific to assume duties assisting the front line units in Vietnam. She would be gone approximately six months. Captain Ware was in command, and most of the crew members who had made the previous cruise were still onboard. So we had a crew of seasoned veterans on our ugly little working ship.

Before we left Hawaiian waters, we picked up a rather interesting towing assignment. We then set sail for WESTPAC, with a couple of stops on our itinerary before we would arrive in Subic Bay. Because of our assignment, we were to make a stop at Midway Island for refueling. If Ute were traveling alone, we would not stop for fuel, because the Ute had huge fuel tanks and could probably go half-way around the world with the fuel on board. We sometimes good heartedly called ourselves a "floating fuel farm." But we would be putting a lot of miles on the Ute before she arrived in Subic, so we set a course for Midway Island. In reality, the refueling was actually for the guys we were towing, and I will discuss them in a bit.

Those of you who know your history will recall that the famous naval Battle of Midway took place in the waters around Midway Island, and with the victory of the United States Navy in that battle, Japan's naval capabilities in World War II were drastically, cripplingly changed. But what you should also know is that Midway Island is just a tiny speck in the ocean. As they say, blink your eyes, and you will miss it.

So the navigator (yours truly) charted our course for Midway, had the course approved by Captain Ware, and we were on our way. It would take several days to reach Midway, and we were enjoying rather calm seas as we charted our celestial navigation throughout the course of each day.

Every evening before leaving the bridge, I would confer with the CO and write the night orders for the OODs. The night orders consisted of instructions that the OODs were to follow through the night hours. They included the speed and course of the ship during the night hours, engineering plant instructions, and navigational instructions. On the night prior to reaching Midway, I wrote the ship's night orders for the OOD's, designating the required course to follow and the exact speed to be maintained as we made our way through the night. In addition, I wrote that there was a navigational light on Midway that should be sighted dead ahead of the ship at approximately 0300 in the morning, the day we were to arrive at Midway. And finally, I wrote that I wanted to be awakened when the light was sighted. I hit my bunk at about eleven p.m. I slept through the night, and at one point I rolled over and checked the time. It was 0500 (5 a.m.). I thought for a moment and remembered that we were supposed to see the Midway light at 0300, and here it was now 0500. Why hadn't I been alerted? I jumped out of my bunk, got dressed, and headed for the bridge and chart house.

As I reached the bridge, it was dark except for the red reading lights and the eerie green glow of the radar repeater situated in the middle of the bridge. Red lights are used on the ship's bridge at night because normal white lights will disable a person's ability to see well in the dark.

When my eyes had adjusted to the dark, I greeted LTJG Pat, the duty OOD, and checked the ship's course. We were on course, but the weather was a bit hazy, so visibility was limited. I looked at the radar repeater to see if it was picking up any land mass, but there was nothing on radar except normal wave action. I then asked the OOD if he had seen the navigational beacon on Midway. He replied that he had not. This was disturbing. We were already two hours past my estimate of when we should have seen the light. What could have gone wrong? I began a slow, growing, panic. Midway was just a speck on the chart, and it would be so easy to miss in a gigantic ocean. The Ute was also a mere speck in the ocean, and it was easy to imagine one speck NOT running into another speck in this huge playing field. The clock kept ticking.

At the appropriate time, the haze had lifted, and we shot our morning stars, fixing our position on the chart. It appeared that we were right on course, but somewhat further from Midway than our earlier predictions. Then again, celestial navigation is not infallible and maybe our fix was not accurate. An inner voice kept saying, "How did I screw this up?" Midway still did not show up on our radar, but that was not surprising, considering the sea state and the low elevation of the island.

At 0600, I figured I had waited long enough and sent a messenger to the captain's cabin with a message that the XO respectfully requested that the captain join him on the bridge. Oh, how I dreaded that! In a few minutes, the CO came to the bridge and asked me how everything was going. I briefed him on our missing island of Midway. Surprisingly, he did not seem upset. He paced the bridge a moment, and I was expecting a salvo at any second, but he calmly sat in his chair and gazed ahead. At 0700, we were now four hours past the time we had predicted to sight Midway, and I was a nervous wreck. All my credibility as a hot shot celestial navigator was flowing down the crapper. I was as low as I could get. I seriously thought that in the earlier low visibility, we may have steamed right by Midway without seeing the navigational light. But Captain Ware still did not panic, and we maintained our course and speed. There was really nothing we could do at this point. I could not understand what might have gone wrong in our calculations, and I was disgusted at myself and my navigation team. Soon, 0730 came, and then 0800, and it was now fully light. Suddenly at 0830, our lookout spotted a light, along with a dark gray, low mass on the horizon. Wow! The ancient navigation gods, who had watched over so many ancient mariners, had just smiled on me. It was our missing island of Midway.

Captain Ware turned to me and said, "See, nothing to worry about."

Well, that was easy for him to say, but I was covered with sweat and guiding the ship across thousands of miles of ocean was my responsibility. I had been about to throw myself overboard and let the sharks end my humiliation. Even as we approached Midway, I fleetingly thought this may be some other island and still thought we may have steamed by an unseen Midway earlier. But thankfully, we soon pulled into the real Midway for our refueling stop with no further incident.

We later concluded that with ocean currents, and our tow behind us, we were not making the speed we had anticipated, and therefore, we were further from Midway than we had predicted. This is a common navigation foible, but it sure got my attention. My reputation as a navigator was, thankfully, salvaged.

Gun Boat Diplomacy

The tow that we had picked up in Pearl Harbor at the start of our journey to WESTPAC was quite out of the ordinary. We were to accompany three coastal gun boats to Indonesia. As such, we were to be U.S. Navy ambassadors to this group of Indonesian Navy personnel who were manning the boats, and we had been instructed to assist them in any way that we could.

The Indonesian Navy had purchased these three gun boats from Germany and were sailing them to Indonesia. They were really neat little ships, bristling with lots of armament, and they looked like mini destroyers. An Indonesian Navy Commander, who was the commodore of the coastal gun boats in his country, was traveling along and riding in one of the boats. Our job was to keep them company, and if any of them experienced mechanical problems while underway, we would take that boat in tow to continue our journey to Surabaya, Indonesia. On the way to Midway, one or two of the boats did break down, and we took them in tow. After breaking down, and while still being towed by us, the Indonesians would work on their boat. When they had the boat operating again, they would signal us, and we would stop to break the tow rig, cutting them loose to proceed on their own power. One boat in particular could not seem to keep running under its own power, so we always had at least one boat in tow, and at one point all three of them were being dragged behind us across the sea! This could have been quite comical and would have made a good episode for "McHale's Navy," but for the fact that it was a great deal of work for our sailors to rig and unrig the towing gear nearly once per day. Hmm, do you think this slow progress may have entered into our delay in finding Midway?

At our fueling stop in Midway, we unrigged our tow and let the gunboats be brought into the pier by the local small tug in Midway. While we were tied up and all the boats were being fueled, it gave us a chance to check out all the towing rigs on the gun boats to be sure that nothing was chafing or damaged. All checked out fine.

Our Midway hosts asked us to join them for lunch, so Captain Ware and I made our way off the ship. We then had the opportunity to see the famous Gooney birds of Midway. The Gooneys are very large birds, with their heads at human crotch level when they are protectively sitting on their nests on the ground; a rather menacing position as Captain Ware and I walked no more than two feet from them as we made our way to lunch. The albatrosses are protected by law, and they are all over the island. Our Midway hosts advised us that when the birds are nesting, they become very protective and have been known to attack a person who ventures too close to the nest. We carefully walked among them as we made our way to the port office and back, with thankfully, no problems.

After fueling had been completed, the Ute, the momma duck, led her little duckling gunboats from the harbor, and we began our course for Guam, our next refueling stop. We played our game of, "take 'em in tow," and then "let 'em go," over and over as we made our way to Guam. I think this was embarrassing to the Indonesian Navy guys, because they just couldn't keep all three boats running for any extended period of time. It would have been ever so much easier if we could have just towed all three of them, all of the time, rather than the aforementioned nonsense. We arrived in Guam and stayed overnight while more repairs were made and refueling was completed.

The next day, we left Guam with three gun boats under their own power trailing behind. Of course, that did not last long, and we soon resumed our towing and releasing routine as the gun boats kept breaking down and getting fixed while under tow. Each time this happened, it meant that our crew had to rig all the towing gear on the Ute and also rig the small disabled ship for towing. This routine was not only maddening, but took a great deal of time and hard work on our part. Our patience was wearing thin, but, diplomacy was the order of the trip, so our crew cheerfully (?) carried out its duty.

We set a generally southwest course to pass to the east of the southern Philippine Island of Mindanao. From there we would continue southwest into the Celebes Sea, through the Makassar Strait, and into the Java Sea as we made our way to Surabaya. I mention these transit points, because this passage would be significant for me and many of the crew members. The course would take us across the equator before reaching Indonesia. Seasoned Navy (and Marine) veterans reading this will immediately know the significance of the equator crossing.

Pollywogs Versus Shellbacks

It is an ancient tradition in the U.S. Navy, the Marines, the Coast Guard, and some other navies of the world, that an elaborate initiation rite is held for those sailors crossing the equator for the first time. Sailors who have previously crossed are known as Trusty Shellbacks, or Sons of Neptune. Sailors who have not yet been initiated are looked upon with scorn and are called Slimy Pollywogs. Because I had never been across the equator, I was a Slimy Pollywog. Not only that, I was the XO of the ship and second in command, I was the most nefarious and evil of all the Slimy Pollywogs and obviously the leader of that scummy group of low life. As such, I would be dealt with in a most appropriate manner by the glorious order of Shellbacks on the Ute. I was not sure what I was in for in my initiation, but I was not about to take this without having my own fun.

The day before the actual initiation is usually Pollywog Day. This is the day for the Pollywogs to "take control of the ship" and generally run amok. In effect, it is a reversal of roles, whereby the lowly Pollywogs take over running the ship instead of the senior members of the crew. Of course, this is all a game, and at no time does the real control of the ship change.

I had gathered together the senior members of the pollywogs to plan our strategy. We would do whatever we could to make life a bit gloomier for the Shellbacks, before they had their chance the next day. First, since all of the chiefs except one were Shellbacks, the Pollywogs put a hasp and padlock on the Chief's quarter's door, so they could not enter their berthing area. Then, we found out where the Shellbacks were making plans for our initiation and learned where their initiation props were being kept. We broke into that storage locker and threw their props over the side of the ship. Next, we went into the galley and gathered up all of the garbage cans we could find and emptied them over the side. (You will know why in a moment.) We also found all of the paint and grease cans on the ship and locked them up. Of course, the Shellbacks were just as ingenious as us Pollywogs, so they were able to quickly undo our mischief. (In a moment, you will know why we locked up the paint and grease.) We then took over all the fire hose stations on the ship and soaked down any Shellback who ventured out onto the deck of the ship. Our siege against the Shellbacks continued all of that day and into the night with more Pollywog pranks. By the end of the day, the Shellbacks were thoroughly hacked off and would be ready for us the next day.

As we crossed over the equator the next day, the initiation began. The control of the ship reverted back to the senior Shellbacks, and we Pollywogs were unceremoniously gathered up for our initiation. We were told to wear shorts, boondocker boots, and tee shirts. My band of fellow Pollywogs started the day by being served a royal Davy Jones breakfast of raw eggs, raw hot dogs, and moldy bread. In other words, we had no edible breakfast. We were all then forced to the bow of the ship and tied to various deck fixtures so that we could not hide anywhere on the ship. And then the same fire hoses were turned on our group, to "wash away our disgusting slime."

After we were soaking wet with salt water, King Neptune, with his sidekick Davy Jones, appeared dressed in appropriately outrageous outfits. These two characters then pulled out rolled up scrolls, and Davy Jones began reading the charges against the Pollywogs: "Disrespect for Shellbacks, Carrying out Disgusting Acts of Treason against the Order of Shellbacks," and other humorous charges. At last, they reached the charges against the leader of the Slimy Pollywogs, yours truly. The charges against me included a whole laundry list of humorous charges, and I was portrayed as an arch villain plotting against the solemn order of King Neptune's Realm. Through it all, everyone was laughing and having a good time, but then it became a bit more serious. All of the Pollywogs were untied, and we were ordered to run laps around main deck of the ship. The Shellbacks each held short pieces of fire hose, and as we passed them, we received a whack with a fire hose from each of them. We were forced to run several laps around the ship and were whacked all the while we ran. All of this was happening while the ship was taking its usual forty-or-more degree rolls as it progressed toward Indonesia. It was all I could do just to remain standing, not to mention trying to run and getting smacked with fire hoses while running. We were again tied on the forecastle deck of the ship and more charges were read against us.

Lunch time rolled around, and the Pollywogs were served a cup of salt water and another piece of moldy bread. (The galley must have been saving up that bread for weeks!)

The initiation continued into the afternoon. The shellbacks had made a long tube out of sewn naugahyde. The tube was about twenty feet long, and it was filled with several weeks' worth of ship's galley garbage. I guess we did not find all the garbage on Pollywog Day. The long vinyl tube was laying out on the fantail of the ship, and the garbage was "super ripe." The odor was overwhelming.

Each Pollywog was led to the fantail, where King Neptune and Davy Jones would again read the charges against the Pollywog. The Royal Baby (one of the chubbier senior sailors) sat next to Davy Jones. After that, the poor Pollywog was forced to crawl on hands and knees through the garbage chute. The Pollywog was then brought back to kneel before the Royal Baby and swear allegiance to the Order of the Shellback and King Neptune's realm. After the Pollywog affirmed his allegiance, he was ordered to kiss the Royal Baby. Did I fail to mention that the Royal Baby was wearing only a pair of undershorts and his entire belly was covered in black axle grease? So each Pollywog was forced to kiss the Royal Baby's belly, resulting in all Pollywogs' faces being covered with black axle grease.

Remember, we were accompanying the three gun boats to Indonesia at this time. The boats that were running on their own had pulled up beside us on both our port and starboard sides and were holding those positions as we traveled. The crews on those three gun boats were all hanging over the rails of their little ships watching and taking pictures of this hilarious, and very strange, ceremony taking place on the Ute's main deck. They were laughing, pointing at us, and carrying on, and I think they enjoyed the craziness just as much as our Shellbacks.

Finally, it was my turn. I was escorted to the fantail and brought before King Neptune, Davy, and Baby, and my outrageous discretions were again read to me. I had to kiss the Royal Baby for my first penance. More charges were read (I was apparently a very bad Pollywog), and then I was made to crawl through the garbage chute. I was now covered in wretchedly disgusting garbage, and my face was covered in thick, black axle grease. Again I was brought before Davy Jones, more charges were read (they sounded strangely familiar by this time), and I had to again kiss the Royal Baby and crawl through the chute. Since I was the lead Slimy Pollywog, my treatment was more severe, and I ended up going through the chute and kissing the Royal Baby three times. All the Pollywogs were marched to the fantail, and we were thoroughly hosed down with the fire hoses, primarily to remove the disgusting garbage from all of us. The ceremony concluded with King Neptune and Davy Jones declaring that we were all now fit to join the Royal Order of Shellbacks.

All in all, I think our Ute Shellbacks were a reasonable lot, and we did not suffer too much. We all had a lot of fun carrying out this very old Navy tradition. We were now all members of the experienced military group known as the Shellbacks.

Surabaya At Last

As we approached Surabaya, we had one of the little ships in tow. The Indonesian Commodore asked Captain Ware if we could delay entering Surabaya while his crew made last minute repairs so that all three ships could enter the harbor under their own power. After all, how would it look if the Commodore delivered the newest acquisition of the Indonesian Navy at the end of a towing cable? Face must be preserved! We agreed, and soon all three of the little ships took off on their own power. We followed them into the harbor and were guided to a pier by a pilot. We had arrived safely, and the Indonesian Navy had three new gun boats.

At that time, the Indonesian Navy had a reputation for buying used ships from navies around the world. These three gun boats had come from Germany, but one of Indonesia's primary sources for combatants at that time was Russia. Unfortunately, spare parts for the Russian ships were, apparently, very hard to obtain. As a result, as we passed through the harbor, we saw rows of rusting, non-operable old Russian destroyers and other combatants tied up at the piers. Sadly, these old girls would probably never see action again and would slowly rust away, only to be sold for scrap metal.

Surabaya was one of Indonesia's primary naval bases, and the gun boat Commodore was based here. Because it was unusual to have a U.S. Navy ship visit Surabaya, the Commodore had arranged to have a banquet to honor his American friends and to celebrate the safe journey of the new ships to his country. That evening, everyone except the Ute duty section, attended a lavish dinner held in our honor. Needless to say, the food was exotic to us, and we often had to ask our hosts to identify the food we were eating. But it tasted good, and we enjoyed it very much.

After the dinner, the Commodore asked Captain Ware and me to accompany him to his home in Surabaya. It was an unexpected measure of hospitality for the Commodore to invite us to visit his home. I looked forward to seeing his neighborhood and having a glimpse of the way he and his family lived. We were met at his home by his very gracious wife, and we enjoyed an evening of drinks and conversation with our hosts. The next day, the Ute cast off her lines and once again headed to sea for the very long voyage back to Subic Bay.

Stop Pulling Me Around

Most of our tows back and forth to Vietnam were rather uneventful, and that is the way we liked them. But once in a while, something would occur to make things a bit more challenging. In one instance, we had left DaNang and were returning to Subic Bay. We were towing a floating crane to the shipyard at Subic. Floating cranes are designated by the amount of lift, in tons, they can accomplish. For instance, a crane might be a ten ton crane or a fifty ton crane, etc.

The size of the crane platform is also relative to the lifting capacity of the crane; the greater the capacity, the larger the floating platform. This particular crane was very large, with the floating base of the crane approximately thirty feet wide and sixty or seventy feet from front to back. We had rigged our tow line to connect to deck padeyes at the middle of the front deck of the crane base.

Before we left DaNang, we checked on the weather forecast for our trip across the South China Sea. We were told to expect some rain and storms in our journey. During the next day or two, the wind really picked up, accompanied by a driving rain. The Ute was rolling, and we kept a watch on our crane in tow, as it rolled about and struggled over the swells. Suddenly, we all heard a thunderous cannon-like noise throughout the ship. The tow line had parted, and our floating crane was now loose and drifting. The Ute's huge tow cable was hanging down under the ship. This is extremely dangerous, because that large cable could become entangled in the ship's screw and totally disable the ship. The Ute's engines were stopped, and the process of recovering the cable began. Meanwhile, the seas became even more angry, and the ship was rocking and rolling violently while the deck crew pulled in the tow cable. Our floating crane continued its lurching glide away from us. At last the tow cable was on board, and the Ute began the chase-down of the crane. As the white capped waves washed over the bow of the ship, we continued steaming toward our wayward charge. Because of the sea state, it would be a real problem to launch our whaleboat into the water and pass sailors over to the crane once the ship caught up to it.

Launching a whaleboat is tricky enough, but with huge waves and a violently rocking ship added to the equation, this becomes a very dangerous venture. In seas such as these, life in a whaleboat also is treacherous. As we caught up to the crane, a crew was selected for the whaleboat and while the ship went bow-in to the waves, the boat was laboriously lowered into the water, its motor was started, and lines were cast off for it to make its way to the crane. With each wave, the whaleboat disappeared into a low trough, resurfacing again before the next wave hit. But it continued its approach to the crane platform. I marveled to see the skill of these unsung heroes as they risked their lives to bring the small boat close to the crane. After several dangerous near miss attempts, the boatswain's mate chief and a sailor were able to nimbly scramble out of the whaleboat and onto the crane. Upon examination, they determined that the welded deck padeyes on the bow of the crane had simply pulled off in the raging sea. There were also padeyes on each side of the crane platform. We would need to use these side padeyes for the tow. A bridle cable would be used to reach between the side padeyes. The bridle cable could then be fastened to our tow line. But first, the bridle and the tow cable would have to be sent over to the crane for fastening. This would not be an easy feat in the stormy, windy conditions with huge seas.

While the deck crew rigged the bridle and tow cable, the gunners mate readied a shot line. This particular shot line was on a spool, fastened to a special rifle. The gun contained a type of dart with the end of the shot line attached. The objective was to shoot the dart from the gun over to the crane, and the attached shot line would follow along with the dart. Once the shot line is controlled at both ends between the ship and the barge, a larger diameter line is tied to the shot line, and is dragged across to the barge. Then a larger line is tied to the end of the second line, and it is dragged across. Finally, a larger diameter rope is sent over to the crane, and this rope is wrapped around a capstan on the barge, with the other end attached to the tow cable. In this manner, the huge, heavy tow cable is reattached to the barge for rigging.

The gunners mate took aim and fired the rifle. Immediately, the wind caught the dart, and the shot was far wide and missed the crane. A second shot line was readied, and the gunners mate fired again. It was another clean miss. With only two of these special shot lines remaining on the ship, things were getting tense. The gunners mate waited and waited for a lull in the wind, and he got it. He fired, and we all held our breaths. It looked like another miss, but then the wind caught the projectile and blew it into the crane's structure. The boatswains mate on the crane scrambled into the crane's rigging and retrieved the line. Next, the guys on the crane began trying to start the motor for the crane capstan.

An hour of tinkering with the balky motor passed, and finally, with a huge plume of black smoke, the old engine started. As the heavier lines moved across to the crane, the capstan groaned under the load, but ever so slowly the tow cable with its bridle snaked through the raging waters. This action also pulled the crane closer to the ship. After a couple more hours of back breaking work, the men on the crane had attached all the cables. The runaway crane was once again under our control.

The seas did not diminish. The dangerous task of recovering the small crew from the crane, getting them back into the whaleboat, and bringing the whaleboat back onboard the Ute still remained. The boat coxswain tried his best in the giant whitecaps to get the boat close enough to the barge for the crew to board. My words cannot describe how dangerous this situation was. While the crane was being rapidly pushed to and fro by the wind and waves, the boat coxswain was attempting to bring a boat which was lurching up and down in the swells and also being pushed haphazardly about by the wind and waves, alongside the crane platform to pick up the chief and sailor. A miscalculation by him could smash the boat against the crane and put it out of commission. The Ute only carried one whaleboat. A miscalculated jump into the whaleboat by the chief or the sailor could result in injury or worse. After several hair-raising attempts, the coxswain was successful, and the guys were able to jump aboard the small bucking boat. The coxswain was then able to bring the boat alongside the ship, and the wildly swinging slings were attached to the boat. The boat crew stayed in the boat as it was slowly raised and finally secured to the ship.

Once again, these were unsung heroes doing life threatening work for their nation. The only mishaps were some nasty bruises which occurred when the men fell on the crane platform, and from entering and exiting the whaleboat. We were lucky there were no broken bones or more serious injuries, and we were glad to rid ourselves of the reluctant floating crane when we reached Subic Bay.

God Wakes Us Up
The Ute was scheduled for another R&R trip to Hong Kong in the spring of 1972. I was looking forward to this trip, because I had arranged for Jan to meet me in Hong Kong when the ship arrived. We had reservations in a nice hotel and would play tourist, shop, and just have a great time enjoying each other's company after being apart for so long.

The ship left Subic Bay for Hong Kong with all hands looking forward to a great liberty port, with wonderful sights to see and lots of opportunities to spend money. We kept up with the weather reports for our transit, and we knew that there was a possibility we could be heading into some tropical storms. As we progressed, the seas became rougher and rougher. Then the rains came, accompanied by winds that became steadily stronger. As time passed, we found ourselves in near typhoon weather. Conditions on the ship became miserable. No hot food could be served, and it really would not have mattered if we had had the food, as almost everyone on board became seasick.

The bridge crew tied ropes around themselves and fastened the ropes to the overhead steel bars on the bridge. The ship was not only taking steep and frightening rolls, but it was porpoising too. The bow of the ship went down so deep in the wave troughs that monstrous waves were crashing on the front wall of the pilot house and onto the bridge windows. That meant that the waves were as high as a four story building. When the bow plunged down, the entire stern of the ship came up out of the water, including the propeller. The bow would then rise until the forward half of the ship was out of the water, revealing the forward keel of the ship.

As I mentioned, nearly everyone was seasick. We had tied buckets in various locations around the ship because of the prevalent seasickness. The crew would utilize these buckets to vomit into while they tried desperately to carry out their assigned duties. The sailor on the ship's wheel had a bucket tied to the compass next to him and was periodically retching into the bucket. The stench on the bridge was overpowering. The only person who may not have been sick was Captain Ware. He placed his Captain's chair on the bridge in the full recline position and did not move out of the chair except when absolutely necessary.

Normally, the ship was a very loud place in its own right. The engines and machinery constantly provided a high decibel background twenty-four hours of every day while underway. But the constant freight train noise of the storm succeeded in drowning out the internal ship's noises. The wind shrieked wildly, and the ship's superstructure whined eerily as the gale blew through the wires and antennae. The driving rain was horizontal, and visibility was down to zero. We could not see past the bow of the thrashing ship.

In a situation of greatly diminished visibility, maritime rules state that a ship will periodically blow its ship's horn, which is normally very loud, to warn other ships in the vicinity. Usually this is no big deal, but the torrential, horizontal driving rain had somehow gotten into the inner workings of the whistle, thereby making it inoperable. It only gave off a weak squeaking noise. For just this reason, the ship carried a hand operated whistle. So, we placed a man on the lookout deck, who began operating a hand air pump connected to this back-up whistle. Alas, in all the noise of the storm, that whistle was even more feeble. It would not have been an especially good time to suddenly meet another ship at sea.

Because we could not see the horizon, sun, or stars, celestial navigation was out of the question. We had to rely on dead reckoning, which was nearly useless considering the wind, sea state, and our marginally working LORAN Charlie. I was never very good with that contraption, and the quartermaster chief and one of the warrant officers assumed the duty of trying to get a navigational fix with it.

While on watch on the bridge, we constantly were mesmerized by the bridge clinometer as it madly swung back and forth, and we recorded regular rolls of forty-eight degrees, plus. Unlike most storms that we had experienced, which had lasted generally a day or less, this one was a real gale of near hurricane proportions, lasting more than three days. The South China Sea was living up to its reputation as being one of the roughest bodies of water in the world. When the crew was off duty, they would try to sleep, but this was almost impossible in these horrendous conditions. When crew members climbed into their bunks, they used straps that could be attached to the edge of the bunk, passed over their bodies, and attached to the other side of the bunk to keep them from being violently thrown into the bunk above them or ejected onto the deck below. In my own bunk, I curled up into a corner and ran a rope over my body which was fastened on each side of the bunk to tie myself in, but sleep would last no more than a few minutes. Even though my body was thoroughly worn out from fighting the rolling ship, I would be rudely awakened every couple minutes by the violent heaving of the ship. Meals could not be prepared, and as a result the ship's supply of "sea cookies" (saltine crackers) was soon exhausted, as the men tried to keep something in their stomachs.

At one point in the storm, more out of curiosity than anything else, I made my way to the fantail of the ship, four decks below the bridge, to watch the effects of the storm and the struggles of our little ship. The visual effects were frighteningly awesome from that level on the ship. The fantail would rise to the point that the ocean was not visible on either side of the ship. The stern would then violently shudder and lower in a heart-stopping free fall, so that it was then in an angry, undulating canyon of water with walls of waves rising far above each side of the ship. As I held myself braced against some machinery on the fantail and looked out on both sides of the ship, all I could see was a four story wall of water on each side of the ship, and the fantail was awash in sea water. At this point, I realized I was a damn fool for being on the fantail at all. In this storm I could easily be washed overboard. I quickly made my way back to the bridge.

This was the first time since I had joined the Ute that I truly became concerned for our valiant little ship and its crew of unsung heroes. Man makes a ship, and God makes a monster storm. At that point, I had a genuine concern that maybe God would take our mortal lives. To compound that thought, I remembered that the Ute had seen duty in 1946, in and around the Yangtze River in China. In October of that year, she had hit a mine, which very nearly separated the aft third from the rest of the ship and completely crippled her to the point that she, herself, had to be towed back to the west coast of the United States from China.[25] Therefore, the Ute had been mortally wounded before. Although she had been rebuilt in 1946, I gave considerable thought to whether or not the man-made rivets holding the steel plates together throughout the ship would be able to withstand such a severe beating from this devilish force of nature.

The storm raged for three days. Near the end of the storm, the entire crew looked like refugees from a zombie nation. For three days, no one had eaten, no one had clean or dry clothes, no one had shaved, and everyone was so tired they could barely walk. We were physically, seriously beat up. We were a wet, haggard lot, and we looked like we had just been released from a prison camp. Meanwhile, the Ute continued to struggle on through the unrelenting seas and doggedly kept her old round bow pointed toward our Hong Kong goal.

In the afternoon two days before we were to arrive in Hong Kong, the storm broke, and the sky began to clear, with bright sunlight and a slowly subsiding ocean. Our stout, little ship had persevered and carried us all to safety. I personally marveled at the strength of the Ute and praised those American ship builders who had carefully constructed and later repaired the Ute. And I thanked God for our safety.

We took our navigation fixes by celestial readings that evening, and discovered that we had predictably wandered from our course. We would be able to recover our lost ground during the following day, leaving us only a few hours behind our scheduled arrival. It had been a trip that none of us would forget.

After our five day transit, we arrived in Hong Kong harbor, picked up our pilot, and moved to our berth. During our stay, we would be anchored out in the harbor. We would also provide a berth for an American submarine that, like the Ute, was also visiting Hong Kong. The submarine was tied up to the Ute, with our anchor serving both ships. This was the second time that a sub had tied up next to us, but I had never been aboard a U.S. submarine. I wanted to see the interior of the sub and obtained permission from their CO to have a tour. We were shown through the submarine, and I was impressed. But when I stepped back aboard the Ute, where I could see the ocean around me and the beautiful sky, I was glad I was in the surface Navy.

In my time away, I missed Janet so much. I could not wait to see her and give her a big hug and kiss. As soon as I could leave the ship, I caught our whaleboat and went into the pier at Hong Kong. I then made my way to the Hilton, where Jan was waiting for me. As soon as I entered the room, the overpowering fatigue hit me. I was so tired that I collapsed and slept for several hours before I began to feel human again.

Captain Ware had given me five days of leave time, which I greatly appreciated. As the ship's Captain, he was provided with a car and driver for his use while the Ute was in port. Captain Ware generously allowed me to use the car and its driver, Timmy, who became our guide. What a great opportunity for Jan and me. With Timmy serving as our guide, we visited all of the tourist points, and some places that only Timmy was familiar with. We even walked up to the Communist Chinese border, where Jan had her picture taken with the armed Communist Chinese soldier guarding the gate. We relished our short time together. We ate too much and spent too much money, but we would never have that opportunity again.

Our stay in Hong Kong passed too quickly, and I soon kissed my bride good-bye and headed back to the ship. Jan would fly back to Honolulu the next day. The Ute and its crew set a course back across the South China Sea to Subic Bay. Happily, our return trip was nowhere near as exciting as the previous journey.

Perspective

Many times when I was not with the CO, I would stand along the ship's rail alone. With the constant noise of the ship's machinery and the close confines with my shipmates, I often needed a bit of time by myself to relax and "freewheel" my thoughts. In these rare moments alone, I would gaze out past the stern of the Ute and marvel at the immensity of God's ocean. We all know that the earth is approximately two-thirds water, and when you cross earth's oceans, you begin to get the perspective of that fact. It was a humbling experience to be on a small ship in the middle of the sea with no familiar land formations in sight, yet you know that there is another immense world beneath the ocean's surface, and you are an intruder in that world. Nothing but a heaving blue-green ocean and a blue sky canopy as far as I could see in all directions. At times like that, I would realize how very trivial our human lives are here on earth. We are but mere specks in a huge universe, and yet we humans tend to magnify the importance of our little lives. Ride a small boat in a huge, angry ocean some time, and your perspective will be altered. You will learn humility. You will realize that your fragile life can be snatched from you in an instant, and no matter how invincible you think you are, you will come to realize differently. I believe that every mariner comes to these feelings.

Spending weeks at sea taught me that each day of your life should be viewed as a gift, and that through no fault of your own, it is not necessarily automatic that you will have a future to enjoy. Although we are responsible for our lives and actions to some extent, we should always be mindful there are more powerful forces at work in the universe than we mere humans.

Final Ports
During my last few weeks on the Ute, we settled into our normal routine. We remained based in Subic Bay, but travelled back and forth to Vietnam, pulling disabled water craft back to the ship yards in Subic. We did have one project, though, that meant going to yet another foreign country. We received orders to tow a repaired water craft to Sasebo, Japan. The joint Japanese and American navy base at Sasebo is located on the Japanese southern island of Kyushu. From Subic, this is a distance of nearly 1,400 miles, as the crow flies. With the Ute's maximum speed with a tow of about ten knots, it would require six days or more to reach our destination, depending upon sea conditions, weather, and mechanical reliability. The little ship took these trips as a matter of course, and slowly and methodically churned through the miles at sea.

The unsung heroes in the engineering and deck crews kept the Ute in top working order, and we experienced no serious mechanical difficulties while I was on board. Occasionally, we would have a balky engine or generator, but with a total of four engines and three generators, we could continue functioning while repairs were completed on the inoperative machinery.

Unfortunately, our stay in Sasebo was scheduled for only two days, so we began our return trip to Subic quite soon. This was typical. When we had a working assignment, there was usually a short turn-around in each port, unless it was designated a liberty port for the ship. Then, we could stay a bit longer and play tourist.

Ute continued her unsung hard work in the Western Pacific, and my time on the Ute was coming to a close.

A Life Changing Decision

On my first deployment on the Ute, I had been away from Janet and home for almost five months and nearly that long on this second deployment. I was a full lieutenant, and my tenure with the navy was now three-and-a-half years. If I intended to remain in the Navy for a career, my next duty station would need to be destroyer school in Newport, Rhode Island. Destroyer school, affectionately known as "Destech," is a lengthy course of instruction that prepares junior officers for duty as a department head aboard destroyers or cruisers. Between assignments, while the Ute was idle in Subic, I called my detailer in Washington, D.C. The detailer and I discussed my career and agreed that "Destech" should be my next assignment, and he would find a slot in the school for me. We would talk again in a few days. I then called Janet and asked for her opinion.

She said, "You had every intention of making the Navy your career. You should go ahead and go for it." What a gal!

A couple days later, I again talked to the detailer, and he had indeed, gotten me a quota at the school. Unbelievably, I then told him to cut orders for me to get *out of the Navy*! I had come to the conclusion that being away from my wife and eventual family for a year out of every year-and-a-half was really no way to run a marriage and family. I had decided that I wanted out. I would come to regret that decision later in my life, but I made the decision that made the most sense to me at the time.

A couple of weeks later, I received my orders to leave the Ute and head for San Francisco for out-processing from the Navy.

Home Again

When I left the Ute for the final time in late June 1972, I flew to Hawaii to join Janet and prepare for our move back to the states. While waiting for our move and dates for out-processing, two things happened while we were still in Hawaii that left strong impressions on me.

The Pearl Harbor Officers' Club on weekends was always a fun place to go for a good dinner and some dancing to whatever band might be performing that weekend. On a Saturday night before we left Pearl Harbor, Jan and I went to the O' Club for dinner and to listen to the band. I have two left feet and am a poor dancer, but like many guys who love their wives, I will lovingly make a fool of myself on the dance floor. After our dinner, we adjourned to the dance area where the band was playing. The place was packed. We sat down, and I ordered liquid refreshments for us. We sat talking, sipping our drinks, and listening to the band. I was a happy guy. A large, significant chapter in my life was coming to a close, and we would soon have new adventures. I was with the love of my life, I was feeling mellow, and I was enjoying the music and our conversation. As I gazed out at the dance floor, I watched the happy throng of dancers and reflected upon my Navy career, but soon drew my attention back to the love of my life sitting by my side. I love my wife more than anything in the world, and I believe we think alike. Just being with her that evening, confirmed to me that my decision to leave the Navy was the correct choice for us. The prospect of future separations was a major reason why I was leaving the Naval service. As I previously stated, the Navy is a tough career to have a family. There is also an old saying in the Navy; "The toughest job in the Navy is to be a Navy wife." I believe that.

The other incident occurred while attending an outdoor rock concert near Honolulu, held in the famous Punchbowl crater. The concert was a huge affair, with many different bands playing for two or three days. Entrance to the Punchbowl was on a path through a narrow opening in the crater wall. As Jan and I entered, we saw booths selling all manner of items and several famous bands performing or warming up. We passed thousands of attendees, all dressed in the typical anti-Vietnam war, peace protestors' garb, with long straggly hair, beads, tie dyed clothing, peace symbol necklaces, etc. The odor of burning marijuana was unmistakable as we strolled among the throng of people. With my military haircut, conservative shorts and tee shirt, I received not so friendly stares from others in the crowd. As I listened to various anti-war bands, and then to several stoned, nonsensical, anti-war, haranguing speakers, I was sickened and saddened. I had just completed three and a half years of military duty for my country during an unpopular war. I had done my duty for my country and was proud of it. And yet, here were thousands of young people greatly opposed to the military and our country's role in Vietnam. Their appearance, life style, and attitudes flew in the face of my conservative, Midwest standards of decorum and attitude toward God and country. After a couple of hours, we left the Punchbowl. Later, I struggled inwardly to understand the stance of those folks at the concert. I reached no conclusion, other than that I will never agree with the opinions of those people, and they would certainly never agree with mine. And that conundrum is part of the melting pot experiment, democracy, that we call America. But, had my unsung service to my country during the Vietnam War been a horrible waste of time? I do not believe so. Today, nearly forty years after this incident, I have not changed my mind. I am proud of my military service and proud of every veteran who ever served his/her country in uniform. I salute all the heroes and unsung heroes who toiled in obscurity. I need no convincing that I made the right decision to join the military in 1969.

In July 1972, we flew to San Francisco, where I was honorably discharged from my Vietnam era active duty service. I was once again a civilian. We packed up our car and headed to Iowa, where the next chapters of our lives would begin.

Epilogue

THERE were millions of us who came forward and answered our country's call during the Vietnam War. Sadly, fifty-eight thousand, one hundred forty-eight of those millions gave the ultimate to our wonderful country. Those heroes should never be forgotten. Nor should the thousands of unsung heroes who continued their military careers, or came home to rejoin America's work force and live the American life of freedom and democracy. I salute them all, and especially those unsung heroes mentioned in the book. Their advice, leadership, and friendship meant so very much to me during my active naval service.

After leaving active duty, my wife and I returned to Iowa. We later relocated several times, as we both worked and raised our only son. On our journey of life, I worked as a manager in private industry for fifteen years in human resources and labor relations. I also worked as a manager for the U.S. Government as a civilian for the U.S. Navy, U.S. Customs Service, and Department of Labor, all in human resources and ulcer-inducing labor relations. In our combined careers, we have lived in Iowa; Dallas, Texas; Houston, Texas; San Diego, California; El Paso, Texas; and Fort Worth, Texas.

Twelve years after leaving active duty, I continued to rue my 1972 decision to leave Navy active duty. I missed the military. In 1984, I rejoined the Navy in the reserves. During the course of my reserve duty, I served in numerous commands, as well as being the Commanding Officer for two reserve units. I remained in the reserves for a total of twenty years, rising to the final rank of full commander, at which point I retired. I have given my country twenty years of service in the Navy, and twenty-two years in civilian government service. It has been quite a ride.

I sincerely hope that you have enjoyed the stories in this book. I enjoyed writing them, always with the intent of telling the story of the unsung heroes who served on Navy auxiliary and mine warfare ships; and to honor the military service of some of the unsung heroes whom I met while I served. Bless them all.

I would enjoy hearing from any reader, whether to comment on the book or just to say hello.

Acknowledgements

WHILE writing this, my first book, I have learned a great deal about the difficulty in writing and publishing a book. Much of the learning has been both exhilarating and disappointing. But many people have offered advice and encouragement to me in my progress, and I would like to thank them. My saintly wife, Jan, has been my constant helper and has offered hours of encouragement and editing. My friend LTCOL Jack Drain, author of *Life on a Short Fuse,* has met with me numerous times to offer advice and comment. My brother, Captain Steve Duermeyer, himself an old auxiliary ship sailor, has offered advice and editing. Same with my friend Captain John Williams. I thank these three gentlemen military retirees. I also received comments from Tom Albrecht and Bob Pasquarelli, lasting, real friends from OCS, and from Bill Niblack, my buddy from Charleston days. They have all provided encouragement that kept me going to finish the book. And finally, thanks to Ray Merriam at Merriam Press for having the faith to publish an unknown author. Thank you all.

About the Author

CDR James Duermeyer and his wife Janet live in North Richland Hills, Texas, where their son and grandchildren are close-by. After release from active duty in 1972, he worked in private industry, in Human Resources and Labor Relations Management for fifteen years. During his career, he was the Personnel Director for two different companies. He then entered Government Service, also in Human Resources and Labor Relations, and retired after twenty-two years, all in supervisory and manager positions. His last position was Assistant Regional Administrator in Dallas, Texas, for the Department of Labor. James completed twenty years in the Navy Reserves, holding numerous billets including two Commanding Officer positions, and retired at the rank of Commander. He holds a BA degree from William Penn University in Social Science/Business. This is his first book. He is presently working on a second book, an historical fiction, entitled *Flint Bluff*.

Please visit the author at www.duermeyerbooks.com.